INSPIRATION

ALSO BY DR. WAYNE W. DYER

BOOKS

Being in Balance
Everyday Wisdom
Getting in the Gap (book-with-CD)
Incredible You! (children's book)
Manifest Your Destiny
No More Holiday Blues
The Power of Intention
A Promise Is a Promise
Pulling Your Own Strings
Real Magic
The Sky's the Limit
Staying on the Path
10 Secrets for Success and Inner Peace
There Is a Spiritual Solution to Every Problem
What Do You Really Want for Your Children?
Wisdom of the Ages
You'll See It When You Believe It
Your Erroneous Zones
Your Sacred Self

AUDIO/CD PROGRAMS

Everyday Wisdom (audio book)
Freedom Through Higher Awareness
How to Be a No-Limit Person
How to Get What You Really, Really, Really, Really Want
Inspiration (abridged)
It's Never Crowded Along the Extra Mile
The Keys to Higher Awareness
101 Ways to Transform Your Life (audio book)
Meditations for Manifesting
The Power of Intention (abridged)
A Promise Is a Promise (audio book)
10 Secrets for Success and Inner Peace
The Secrets of the Power of Intention (6-CD set)
There Is a Spiritual Solution to Every Problem
The Wayne Dyer CD Collection
Your Journey to Enlightenment (6-tape program)

VIDEOCASSETTES

Creating Real Magic in Your Life
How to Be a No-Limit Person
The Miracle Mindset in Action
10 Secrets for Success and Inner Peace
What Do You Really Want for Your Children?

MISCELLANEOUS

Inner Peace Cards
Inspiration Cards
The Power of Intention Cards
The Power of Intention Perpetual Flip Calendar
10 Secrets for Success and Inner Peace Cards
10 Secrets for Success and Inner Peace gift products: *Notecards, Candle,* and *Journal*

All of the above are available at your local bookstore, or may be ordered by visiting:
Hay House USA: **www.hayhouse.com**; Hay House Australia: **www.hayhouse.com.au**;
Hay House UK: **www.hayhouse.co.uk**; Hay House South Africa: **orders@psdprom.co.za**

INSPIRATION
YOUR ULTIMATE CALLING

Dr. Wayne W. Dyer

HAY HOUSE
Australia • Canada • Hong Kong
South Africa • United Kingdom • United States

First published and distributed in the United Kingdom by Hay House UK Ltd, Unit 62, Canalot Studios, 222 Kensal Rd, London W10 5BN. Tel.: (44) 20 8962 1230; Fax: (44) 20 8962 1239. www.hayhouse.co.uk

Published and distributed in the United States of America by Hay House, Inc., PO Box 5100, Carlsbad, CA 92018-5100. Tel.: (1) 760 431 7695 or (800) 654 5126; Fax (1) 760 431 6948 or (800) 650 5115. www.hayhouse.com

Published and distributed in Australia by Hay House Australia Ltd, 18/36 Ralph St, Alexandra NSW 2015. Tel.: (61) 2 9669 4299; Fax: (61) 2 9669 4144. www.hayhouse.com.au

Published and distributed in the Republic of South Africa by Hay House SA (Pty), Ltd, PO Box 990, Witkoppen 2068. Tel./Fax: (27) 11 706 6612. orders@psdprom.co.za

Distributed in Canada by Raincoast, 9050 Shaughnessy St, Vancouver, BC V6P 6E5. Tel.: (1) 604 323 7100; Fax: (1) 604 323 2600

Editorial supervision: Jill Kramer • *Wayne Dyer's editor:* Joanna Pyle
Design: Charles McStravick • *Photo of Tysen:* Courtesy of Wayne Dyer

The moral rights of the author have been asserted

A catalogue record for this book is available from the British Library.

ISBN 1-4019-0807-1

Printed and bound in Great Britain by TJ International, Padstow, Cornwall.

For my mother, Hazel Irene Dyer.
You inspire me—
thank you, thank you, thank you!

For Immaculée Ilibagiza.
You could never even imagine
how much better off this world is
because you were "left to tell."
I love you.

CONTENTS

"The highest knowledge man can attain
is the yearning for peace, for the union
of his will with an infinite will,
his human will with God's will."

— ALBERT SCHWEITZER

"Every tree and plant in the meadow
seemed to be dancing,
those which average eyes would see
as fixed and still."

— RUMI

"Let me have the glory with Thee
that I had with Thee even before the beginning."

— JESUS OF NAZARETH

INTRODUCTION

I LOVE BEING INSPIRED, and I trust that the idea of living an inspired life appeals to you as well. I've written this book with the paramount idea of showing you what I've learned about this magical concept.

Writing this book has been a transcendent experience for me. For many months I awoke every morning at approximately 3:30, and after spending my own personal, private moments with God, I sat down to write. Every word of this book was written out long-hand. I'd place my hand on the table and allow the ideas to flow from the invisible world of Spirit through my heart and onto the pages. I know deep within me that I do not own these words—I'm merely an instrument through which these ideas are expressed. I trust in this process, and it works as long as I remain "in-Spirit" while I write. I also trust that these ideas will work for you.

This is the most personal book I've written in my 35 years as an author. I've chosen to use examples from my own life—that is, those I've experienced firsthand. The personal nature of this book is a deliberate choice. I discovered as I went along that, in order to write about such a deeply felt subject as inspiration, I needed to convey what I felt as authentically as possible. Just as one can never actually know what a mango tastes like from another person's description, I wouldn't have been able to adequately convey my familiarity with the experience of inspiration by citing case studies of others. By writing from my heart, I've been able to keep the flavor of inspiration alive here in these pages.

I'm also well aware that I've repeated one theme over and over throughout these pages. I decided not to edit out this repetition because I see this book as an instrument for moving you to a place where you truly understand what it means to be in-Spirit. This oft-repeated theme is: *Live in-Spirit. You came from Spirit, and to be inspired you must become more like where you came from. You must live so as to become more like God.*

One of my favorite mentors and storytellers, Anthony de Mello, was a Catholic priest who lived in India and could convert complex philosophical issues into understandable and simple teachings using the art of storytelling. Here's a short tale from *The Heart of the Enlightened,* in which Father de Mello does such a good job of summing up much of what I want to convey to you about living in-Spirit:

> The devotee knelt to be initiated into discipleship. The guru whispered the sacred mantra into his ear, warning him not to reveal it to anyone.
>
> "What will happen if I do?" asked the devotee.
>
> Said the guru, "Anyone you reveal the mantra to will be liberated from the bondage of ignorance and suffering, but you yourself will be excluded from discipleship and suffer damnation."
>
> No sooner had he heard those words than the devotee rushed to the marketplace, collected a large crowd around him, and repeated the sacred mantra for all to hear.
>
> The disciples later reported this to the guru and demanded that the man be expelled from the monastery for his disobedience.

The guru smiled and said, "He has no need of anything I can teach. His action has shown him to be a guru in his own right."

I trust that the meaning of this story will become clearer and clearer as you immerse yourself in this book. You have a profound calling back to Spirit. It is working right now in your life, otherwise you wouldn't be reading these very words in this very instant. I urge you to heed that calling and come to know the pure bliss that awaits you as you make an inspired life your reality.

In-Spirit,
Wayne W. Dyer

PART I

INSPIRATION—
LIVING IN-SPIRIT

*"A physical body was given him [man]
by Nature at birth. Somewhere exists
the original Divine spark launched
from God and which, refound,
will be his conscious spirit."*

— RODNEY COLLIN
from *The Theory of Conscious Harmony*

CHAPTER 1

LIVING YOUR LIFE IN-SPIRIT

"When you are inspired . . .
dormant forces, faculties, and talents become alive,
and you discover yourself to be a greater person
by far than you ever dreamed yoursef to be."

— PATANJALI

IN THE TITLE OF THIS BOOK, I've deliberately used the word *calling* to indicate the importance of inspiration as it applies to our lives. There's a voice in the Universe entreating us to remember our purpose, our reason for being here now in this world of impermanence. The voice whispers, shouts, and sings to us that this experience—of being in form in space and time—has meaning. That voice belongs to inspiration, which is within each and every one of us.

Inspiration responds to our attentiveness in various and sometimes unexpected ways. For example, when I began writing this book, I debated between the two titles *Inspiration: Your Ultimate Destiny* or *Inspiration: Your Ultimate Calling.* One day while swimming in the ocean, I was going back and forth in my mind, trying out both titles. Still uncertain when I'd finished my swim, I called Reid Tracy, president and CEO of Hay House, the company that publishes my books, from a pay phone to get his opinion about the title. While I waited for him to answer, the word *calling* appeared on the miniature screen of the phone. Nothing else, just *calling*. And then the word began to flash on and off as if it were trying to get my attention.

When Reid answered, I told him what had just occurred, and we both agreed on *Inspiration: Your Ultimate Calling* for the title of my new book. All of this may appear to be nothing more than a silly coincidence, but I know better.

Consider that the word *coincidence* itself relates to the mathematical idea of angles that coincide. When two angles join in this way, they're said to fit together perfectly. Not accidentally—*perfectly*. Any so-called coincidence might then just be an alignment of forces fitting together in flawless harmony. The word *calling* flashing before my eyes, for instance, at the exact moment that I was trying to choose between *calling* or *destiny* exemplifies an opportunity to notice something important. You see, what catches our attention might be more than a coincidence—it might also be a potential incident of inspiration.

We know that there's something deep within us waiting to be known, which we sometimes call a "gut reaction" to life's events. We have a built-in yearning to seek our inspired self and feel wholeness, a kind of inexplicable sense that patiently demands recognition and action. We might describe it as a mechanism persistently projecting the words *destiny, mission,* or *purpose* on our inner screen. It's possible to have our daily behavior so aligned with these inner feelings that we unequivocally know what our calling is. In fact, if you put this book aside and check in with what you're feeling at this moment, my guess is that you'll hear a part of yourself crying out, "Yes, I want to have more inspiration in my life! I want to know my calling!"

I promise you that after your first reading of this book, you'll begin to be intimately connected to your inspired self. I say this with such certainty because it's *my* calling to write and publish these words. You see, *you're* a component of *my* ultimate calling.

I think of the word *inspiration* as meaning "being in-Spirit." When we're in-Spirit, we're inspired . . . and when we're inspired, it's because we're back in-Spirit, fully awake to Spirit within us. Being inspired is an experience of joy: We feel completely connected to our Source and totally on purpose; our creative juices flow, and we bring exceptionally high energy to our daily life. We're not judging others or ourselves—we're uncritical and unbothered by behaviors or attitudes that in uninspired moments are frustrating. Our heart sings in appreciation for every breath; and we're tolerant, joyful, and loving.

Being in-Spirit isn't necessarily restricted to the work we do or the activities of our daily life. We can be inspired and at the same time be unsure of what vocation to pursue or what activities we want to schedule. Inspiration is a simple recognition of Spirit within ourselves. It's a return to that invisible, formless field from which all things emanate, a field of energy that I called "intention" in my previous book *The Power of Intention.*

In *this* book I'm going beyond an understanding of the inherent power of intention, however, by describing how to live in-Spirit and hear the voice of inspiration even when we're doing absolutely nothing that we'd call purposeful. This is quite different from being highly motivated; in fact, it's almost the opposite of motivation.

Motivation vs. Inspiration

It's important to note that whatever is needed to fulfill our calling is part of the present process. Arthur Miller, who was perhaps the most accomplished dramatist in the U.S., is an example of a man who knew this. In an interview late in his life, he was asked, "Are you working on a new play?" Mr. Miller's answer went something like this: "I don't know if I am or not, but I probably am." This delightful response suggests that Miller's writing came from inspiration—that is, something other than ego spurred him on.

By contrast, highly motivated people have a kind of ego determination driving them over obstacles and toward goals—*nothing* gets in their way. Now, most of us have been taught that this is an admirable trait; in fact, when we're not accomplishing and demonstrating drive and ambition, we've been told to "get motivated!" Lectures, books, videos, and audio recordings abound that preach that all we have to do is dedicate ourselves to an idea with actions designed to make it a reality. This is a beneficial approach for a different level of accomplishment—but what we're exploring in these pages is what leads us to precisely what we're meant to be and do . . . our ultimate calling.

If motivation is grabbing an idea and carrying it through to an acceptable conclusion, then inspiration is the reverse. When we're in the grip of inspiration, an idea has taken hold of us from the invisible reality of Spirit. Something that seems to come from afar, where we allow ourselves to be moved by a force that's more powerful than our ego and all of its illusions, is inspiration. And being in-Spirit is the place where we connect to the invisible reality that ultimately directs us toward our calling. Often we can identify these inspired times by their insistence, and because they seem not to make sense while at the same time they keep appearing in our consciousness.

If we ignore inspiration's powerful attraction, the result is personal discomfort or a sense of disconnection from ourselves. For any number of reasons, we might be resistant when we feel called to create, perform, visit a foreign place, meet someone, express ourselves, help another, or be a part of a cause. Inspiration is a calling to proceed even though we're unsure of goals or achievements—it may even insist that we go in the direction of uncharted territory.

Throughout various stages of life, inspiration is the thought or idea reconnecting us to the energy we were part of prior to becoming a microscopic particle. I call this "surrendering to our destiny and allowing ourselves to hear the call." At this point we can differentiate between the demands of our ego and those of the ego-dominated people and institutions that deflect us from the call of inspiration. As we move more deeply into Spirit, we cease to be guided by the ego demands of others or ourselves. We surrender to the always-present force that urges us to be in this blissful state of inspiration. We're guided by our ultimate calling, which is truly our life purpose.

A Force Beyond Even Our Own Life

The invisible reality, where all physical life originates, is more powerful and significant than the tiny parenthesis in eternity that we call "life," or what comes between birth and death. The spiritual dimension of the invisible reality calls to us in this material world of beginnings and endings. This spiritual essence is our Source, which is magnificent and stupendous compared to our earthly self. When we're inspired (as I refer to it in this book), we're connected to this force that's greater in every respect than our physical being. It was in-Spirit that our purpose was laid out, and it's in-Spirit where our magnificence is absolute and irrefutable. Before merging into form, we were a part of God, with all the inherent qualities of a Creator who sends forth abundance, creativity, love, peace, joy, and well-being.

When we feel what Arthur Miller apparently did, we acknowledge and rejoin that more expansive energy field running through us, and we invite this Source to participate in our daily life. We suspend our ego identification and warm to the idea of trusting the energy that created us. We choose to live in-Spirit, entrusting ourselves to something greater than our life as a physical being. When we listen and allow it to, Spirit guides us; when we fail to listen—or allow our ego to get in the way and run the show—we're going to be uninspired. It's that simple.

Later in this book there are specific suggestions for communing with and connecting to this part of ourselves. First, I'd like to share some of the personal experiences I've had when I've been in-Spirit.

My Experience with Being in-Spirit

When I'm in-Spirit, I have a feeling of contentment, but more than this, I experience joy. I'm able to receive the vibrational energies of my Source—call them voices, messages, silent reminders, invisible suggestions, or what have you, but they're vibrations of energy that I'm able to align with as I get myself out of the way. Wolfgang Amadeus Mozart, one of the world's great geniuses, once remarked: "When I am, as it were, completely myself, entirely alone, and of good cheer—say, traveling in a carriage, or walking after a good meal, or during the night when I cannot sleep—it is on such occasions that my ideas flow best and most abundantly. Whence and how they come, I know not, nor can I force them."

We don't have to be a genius to know what Mozart speaks of—the same force in a different way is flowing through you and me right now. I've learned to remove resistance to the free flow of this spiritual energy by reminding myself to align with it, or to be in-Spirit in my thoughts and expectations.

Spirit doesn't dwell on the impossibility of anything—that is, it doesn't focus on not being able to create, on things not working out, on expecting the worst, or on being stuck in place. When I'm in-Spirit, I want my present moment and thoughts to align perfectly with what I desire. I want to offer an experience of inspiration to my audience, so I don't give a speech thinking, *I'll probably disappoint them.* I choose to know that if I stumble or forget something in the middle of my talk, the inspiration to get me through it will be there. The results are exhilarating feelings of inspiration.

When I sit down to write, my desire is to invite Spirit to express through me, and I encourage ideas to flow freely. Like Mozart, I'm connected, as it were, to my Source in-Spirit, thinking and expecting to be the instrument of my spiritual Source. Ideas flow, and whatever assistance I need just shows up. And like Mozart, I can't describe how the ideas come, and I can't force them. Staying in-Spirit seems to be the secret to this feeling of being inspired.

I also find that inspiration flows in other areas of my life when my primary mission is like what Michael Berg so beautifully describes in *Becoming Like God: Kabbalah and Our Ultimate Destiny:* ". . . just as every being is God's business, every being becomes our business as well." That is, being inspired necessitates the willingness to suspend ego and enter a space where I want to share who I am and what I have in a completely unlimited fashion.

At a recent lecture, for instance, a woman named Rolina De Silva approached me at the break to ask if I'd visit her teenage daughter, Alison, in The Hospital for Sick Children in Toronto. Alison had been hospitalized for many, many months due to a rare disease that's characterized by a breakdown of the lymphatic system. Her intestines had been perforated, so she was unable to process proteins and fats . . . and her prognosis was dismal at best.

As I sat with Alison on my third visit with her, I held her hand and noticed that a scab was forming on the top of her hand from a minor injury brought about by an intravenous injection. Something came over me in that moment, and I looked into the girl's eyes and reminded her that the scab was a gift to her. It indicated that the essence of well-being (our Source) was working within her. I reminded her that all she had to do was to summon that same well-being to her abdomen. "You're already connected to Spirit," I almost shouted, "otherwise you wouldn't be growing a scab over that cut on your hand!"

When I spoke with Rolina 14 months later, I asked if she remembered that day in the hospital when I held Alison's hand and felt inspired by the scab. Rolina replied that that day was a new beginning for her daughter, as something inside of her opened. Always before she'd had a blank look on her face, yet she gave off an air of intolerance about the entire process. When the girl realized that she was indeed connected to Spirit, evinced by the presence of the scab forming on her hand, she changed her attitude completely.

Today Alison is back home and actually doing work to raise money for that same hospital where she spent so many months as a critical-care patient. (If you ever see me speaking on television or in person, you'll notice a little angel pin that I wear, which was given to me by Alison as a thank-you gift. To me, this pin is a symbol of the angel that guided me that day to speak to Alison as I did.)

I know in my heart that when we remember we're always connected to this Source and that we can summon the well-being of

God, it is then that we're said to be inspired. Whether the outcome is miraculous, as was Alison's, or our physical reconnection to our Source is completed through the death of our body, we live out our moment in-Spirit. It's important to understand that *each and every one of us represents God or Spirit revealing Itself here on our planet.*

Also, keep in mind that our creative force is a forthcoming energy. I find that when I emulate it, the result is inspiration flowing through my life, and I'm living a life that is my ultimate calling. If I feel called to something higher and then do nothing about it, I'll generally find myself experiencing discontentment and disappointment. But when I act upon that calling by being in vibrational harmony with it, and by being willing to share it with as many people as possible, I feel inspired.

When I donate books to a prison or a library, for example, I feel my ultimate calling being fulfilled by my actions. And just this morning I received a thank-you call from a woman who'd asked me for an endorsement for her work. I'd taken the time to respond with an appraisal of how her spiritual practice of healing hypnosis had benefited me and what I thought it could do for others. She said, "Your words were the greatest Christmas gift I ever received." So why am *I* still inspired by this? Because I left the world of ego and entered the world of expressing Spirit to benefit another person.

These experiences of being in-Spirit are available to all of us—I've simply used some personal vignettes here to illustrate ways to discover the calling for each of us. I've felt called to help others, and my life has taken me in that direction.

In What Direction Are You Moving?

Being in-Spirit is a direction we take, rather than a destination to be reached. Living our life in-Spirit requires us to determine that direction, and we do so by noticing our thoughts and behaviors. Thoughts that are in-Spirit reflect a vibrational alignment moving us toward our ultimate calling—and, obviously, this is the direction we want to take. Once we begin to observe our thoughts, we realize that there are many times we're going in the opposite direction. When we catch ourselves, with conscious effort we can make a U-turn with new thoughts. For example, blaming something we call "evil" is thinking in the wrong direction. When we see things in our world that we label evil, what we're really seeing are people moving away from their Source, not individuals in the grip of an evil power.

In our world there are many activities that seem to be motivated by evil, but we must be careful not to assign power to a force that doesn't exist. There are only people moving away from Source with behavior that contradicts the creative energy that's within them. When we have thoughts that reflect hatred, judgment, and exclusion, we're moving away from our Source. When those non-spiritual thoughts explode in the painful form of terrorist activities, for instance, we call them evil. While the pejorative labels that we use may alleviate our feelings of anger and helplessness, they don't help us be in-Spirit. It's imperative for all who seek an inspired life to assess the direction of their thoughts and behaviors in terms of going toward, or away from, Spirit. Condemning behavior as an evil force is thinking that takes us away from living in-Spirit.

To become inspired on a daily basis, we must be able to quickly identify any thoughts that are moving us away from our Source, and then shift the direction. We need to bring love to the presence of hatred, as Saint Francis advised. When we're consumed with thoughts we've labeled as evil, we need to notice that we're headed in the wrong direction. It's difficult to comprehend because we're accustomed to blaming our problems on external forces such as evil or hate, but we know better. We can make that U-turn by using the same energy within us that has us traveling away from God.

Evil, hatred, fear, and even illness soften with love and kindness when we're in-Spirit. When we make that U-turn, we make an alignment correction and move back into the space of Spirit in our thoughts and actions.

Some Suggestions for Putting the Ideas in This Chapter to Work for You

— Commit to at least one daily experience where you share something of yourself with no expectation of being acknowledged or thanked. For example, before I begin my daily routine of exercise, meditation, or writing, I go to my desk and choose my gift for that day. Sometimes it's just a phone call to a stranger who's written to me, or perhaps I order flowers or send a book or present to someone who has helped me in a local store. On one occasion I wrote to the president of the university I graduated from to start a scholarship fund, on another day I took a calender to the yard man, on another I sent a check to Habitat for Humanity, and on another I sent three rolls of postage stamps to my son who'd just started his own business. It doesn't matter if this activity is big or small—it's a way to begin the day in-Spirit.

— Become conscious of all thoughts that aren't aligned with your Source. The moment you catch yourself excluding someone or having a judgmental thought, say the words "in-Spirit" to yourself. Then make a silent effort to shift that thought to match up with Source energy.

— In the morning before you're fully awake, and again as you're going to sleep, take one or two minutes of what I call "quiet time with God." Be in a state of appreciation and say aloud, "I want to feel good."

— *My life is bigger than I am.* Remind yourself of this statement. Print it out and post it strategically in your home, car, or workplace. The "I" is your ego identification. Your life is Spirit flowing through you unhindered by ego—it's what you showed up here to actualize—and is infinite. The "I" that identifies you is a fleeting snippet.

— Dedicate your life to something that reflects an awareness of your Divinity. You are greatness personified, a resident genius, and a creative master—regardless of anyone's opinion. Make a silent dedication to encourage and express your Divine nature.

* * *

A Course in Miracles quotes Jesus as saying: "If you want to be like me I will help you, knowing that we are alike. If you want to be different, I will wait until you change your mind." Being inspired is truly being like your Source. If you're not, then your Source is politely waiting for you to do something as simple as *change your mind.*

CHAPTER 2

YOUR LIFE BEFORE YOUR BIRTH INTO A BODY

"All bodies emerge from the Soul and return to it.
The visible emerges from the invisible,
is controlled by it, and returns to it."

— LAO RUSSELL

QUANTUM PHYSICISTS TELL US that particles don't create more particles; rather, they're said to proceed from what are described as "waves of energy." And physicists and metaphysicists agree that, in a physical sense, life as we know it springs from an invisibleness that we often call Spirit. I'm sure that it comes as no surprise to you that the invisible world of Spirit from which all physical particles originate isn't explainable or verifiable. Words can't define with precision what's inherently clear to us at moments of *knowing*.

This is clearly a purposeful Universe, with an intelligence supporting its creation and continuing evolution—and we're pieces of that intelligence by virtue of having emerged from it. Consider, for example, that scientific analysis of even a droplet of blood reveals all of the characteristics in our entire body's supply. The percentage of iron in that droplet is proportionately the same as in that which flows through our entire body—so it's easy to agree that the drop of blood is identical to the source from which it was removed.

Now think about what happens to that droplet of blood when it remains in the state of separation: It can't fortify or heal us, and it can't circulate freely. Disconnected from its source long enough, it will simply dry up, decay, and disintegrate, even though it contains all of the physical properties necessary to survive that its original source does.

I believe that our transition from spiritual Source to physical beings made up of particles is similar to that bit of blood in that we contain all of the same properties as our Source—but unlike that droplet, we're never completely separated from our Source. I know that there are no accidents in a Universe directed by a Source energy that creates endless real magic in the form of Its creations. I know that we agreed to move from the world of Spirit into the world of particles and form, to come forth at the exact time that we did, and to leave when we've agreed to do so. I also know that we decided to bring joyful perfection to this world, and to share that God-like energy with everyone we encounter here on Earth. It's our nature to do so!

Ancient mystical traditions teach that our planet exists as a vehicle to share the Creator's universal love, beauty, and abundance. When we leave Spirit, we don't necessarily have to separate from our original nature, but that's what seems to happen. Becoming inspired requires our being curious about, and attentive to, feelings that emerge to help us reconnect with our original self.

Inspiration flowing through us is a messenger from the realm of our nonphysical self, from where we were before we entered this visible world of form. We have the ability to return to that formlessness right now, in our body, without experiencing physical death.

This is largely a mental excursion, which requires us to think in ways that we imagine the All-Creating Energy, or God, thinks. What must it have been like just before we made the transition from Spirit to form? In the infinite oneness that we were (and still are), something took place to allow that aforementioned wave of energy to manifest into a tiny subatomic particle, and then to a quark, an electron, an atom, a molecule, and ultimately a cell that comprised all that we needed for the physical manifestation of our body and all of its pursuits, accomplishments, acquisitions, and physical properties.

Our life before becoming an embodiment of Spirit was exactly like our Source. Then we began the transition process and became a tiny fetus intended to spend nine months developing in our mother's womb. I contend that we've *chosen* to enter this world of particles and form. In ways that we don't readily comprehend now, when we were in our place of origin we knew what we were coming here to accomplish, and we participated in setting this life process in motion.

Why place the responsibility or blame on any *one* or any *thing* that's not a part of us? On Earth we have been given the gift of volition (that is, we can choose), so let's assume that we had the same capacity when we resided exclusively in the spiritual realm. We chose our physical body, just as we chose the parents we needed for the trip. And it doesn't seem too great a stretch to believe that we chose this life in concert with our Source.

The very first particle of human protoplasm intended to be our self wasn't the architect of our physical being—instead, it was an aspect of an invisible, formless energy field that was our self *manifesting*. In the particle, and the energy field from which it emanated, were the size and shape of our eyes, our legs, our mouth, and so on. So it feels intuitively natural to me to assume that in that field of energy, the very shape of our life was also encapsulated.

You see, deep within us lies an awareness of what shape our life is to take. We can hear that voice, the one that wants us to know our calling, if we choose . . . but first we need to surrender to that Divine plan we signed up for before our conception.

Our First Nine Months in Form

Let's take a second to go back to what took place from the first moment of our manifestation into a particle, right up until the instant that we emerged from our mother's womb.

Our embryo became a fetus in a space of total faith and harmony—it had no demands, since it was simply carried along by the Divine forces of nature. The basics of our development occurred without our interference: Our brain developed independent of our ideas about how it should be done; our heart, liver, kidneys, toes, fingers, eyebrows, and every other feature appeared on a schedule that seems miraculous from this side of the womb! For most of us, it was nine months in the hands of the Source of life inside a woman's womb (who may or may not have been welcoming our existence). Whatever energy we needed to grow into the being that we signed up to be flowed directly to and through us.

How could we have gotten along so well in those first nine months with only the cooperation of our mother allowing us to develop inside of her? How could everything we required for the beginning of our human journey be so perfectly aligned with the Creative Spirit? The seed that we came from was so tiny that millions of them could fit on the head of a pin, and it looked identical to the seed that begins a giraffe, a palm tree, or any other living organism. So how did it eventually become you or me?

The seed materialized into what we intended to become under the auspices of the Creative Intelligence, and it flourished with the assistance of that remarkable Spirit that's responsible for all of life. The entire process of creation simply unfolded. . . . During those months that we lived in the womb, it's safe to say that we were in-Spirit—we were allowing Spirit to perfectly align without any effort on our part. We were provided for entirely by a life force that none of us can completely describe or explain. We were a little larvae-shaped ooze ball that, in a relatively short period of time, became a human being with the apparatus necessary to support life outside of the womb.

We can see that there's a force in the Universe that's 100 percent trustworthy, one that we relied upon to get us here. It creates and manifests from a spirit of love, cooperation, beauty, and expansiveness, and it's to this flawless work of Spirit that we can return in order to know inspiration. Throughout our life, we continue our development outside of the womb, wherein we rely on the energy of creation to fuel the light of inspiration within us.

Now I'd like to share a conversation I was privileged to have with my originating Spirit. (As I mentioned previously, this is an exercise that we can all do in our imagination.) It was an amazing experience, which I encourage everyone to seek the opportunity to have, or at least be on the lookout for circumstances that will make it happen.

My Conversation with My Spirit
Before Manifesting into
a Physical Particle

Being in a Universe that's created and guided by an organizing intelligence that precludes accidents and coincidences, I've always felt that my presence here at this time is a component of that intelligent system. In a powerful experience of hypnosis, I re-created a conversation between my highest spiritual self and my originating Source to which I'm still connected. This one imaginary exchange has been exceedingly helpful to me for the major portion of my adult life.

I was conceived on the first day of September in 1939 and born on the tenth day of May in 1940. The day of my conception was the same day that Adolf Hitler invaded Poland; two days later, World War II was initiated. I was born on the same day that the Nazis invaded and occupied Belgium, the Netherlands, and Luxembourg, and I saw the Holocaust coming. I knew that I was to play a dominant role in reversing the kind of hatred that precipitated the horrendous actions that resulted in the slaughter of millions.

I came here to teach self-reliance and compassion, just as in an earlier incarnation in the 13th century when I wandered through Europe and Asia with or as Francesco Bernadone (who later became Saint Francis of Assisi), attempting to stop the vicious activities known as the Crusades. My infinite soul was, and still is, tormented by human beings' inhumanity to their fellow humans and wants to eradicate suffering caused by separating ourselves collectively and individually and using violence to settle disputes. The answer, it seems to me, is to teach others how to connect to their Source and stay in this consciousness of love, peace, kindness, and oneness. When enough of us make this journey back to being in-Spirit, our groups and collectives will reflect the inspiration I'm called to promote in one way or another.

As I readied myself to make the shift from an exclusively spiritual being into the world of particles in 1939, I had the following conversation with the Creative Intelligence I'll call God.

God: What would you like to accomplish on this journey you're about to undertake?

Me: I'd like to teach self-reliance, compassion, and forgiveness.

God: Are you certain this is what you wish to dedicate this lifetime to?

Me: Yes. I can see the need even more clearly now.

God: Well, then, I think we'd better put your little ass into a series of foster homes and have you stay there for a decade or so, where you'll learn to experience relying upon yourself. And we'll remove your parents so that you won't be dissuaded from your mission.

Me: I accept that. But what about my parents? Who will best facilitate my life's purpose?

God: You can select Melvin Lyle Dyer as your father. A prisoner, an alcoholic, and a thief, he'll abandon you as a baby and never show up in your life. You'll first practice hating him and seeking revenge, but you'll ultimately forgive him, long after he's left his body. This act of forgiveness will be the single-most important event of your life. It will put you on the path that you're signing up for.

Me: And my mother?

God: Take Hazel Dyer, Lyle's wife. Her compassion for all of her children will give you an example to follow. She'll steadfastly work herself to the bone to reunite you and your brothers after ten years or so of her own suffering.

Me: Isn't it an awfully cruel fate for my father?

God: Not at all. He signed up for this 25 years ago. He dedicated this entire lifetime to teach one of his children the lesson of forgiveness—a noble gesture, wouldn't you say? And your mother is here to show you how true compassion shows up every day. Now get down there and participate in becoming a particle.

In the Introduction of my book *You'll See It When You Believe It,* I wrote about finding my father and visiting his grave in the early 1970s. The facts that led me there defy the laws of logic—and visiting it was the final hurdle I needed to overcome before initiating my writing and speaking career, or the mission I'd signed up for back in 1939.

I've also visited the Holocaust sites of Europe and read and reread the history of events that contributed to the hatred that created war. In the 1960s I worked to bring peace to the events surrounding the horrible Vietnam War, and today my attention is often focused on finding an alternative to the violence and hatred in Africa, the Middle East, and particularly Iraq. My calling is deep within me and has a hold on me. Like Arthur Miller, I don't know what I'm going to do next, but I'm probably being guided by what Spirit and I decided at the inception of this journey. One thing I know for certain is that I'm inspired!

I've described my personal insight about my calling to encourage all of you to examine your own life—including all of its travails and success—as a necessary experience in order to fulfill your mission. Looking at life from this perspective nurtures the deep yearning within that will beckon you back to Spirit.

Looking at Life from an Inspired Perspective

As you can see from my own example, it can be a great help to look at your entire life as the unfolding of a plan that you participated in before you even arrived here. By doing so, you shift from blaming others and circumstances to being responsible and feeling your purpose. Whatever shows up in your life then becomes a part of the perfection of this plan. When everything you experience seems unwelcome, for instance, you can search for what you gain from the apparent obstacles.

If we can remember that we're responsible for what we're attracting, we can then eliminate the negative energy we wallow in. If what we desire is to be inspired and feel joy, but the opposite keeps showing up, rather than cursing fate, we can view ourselves as simply being out of creative vibrational alignment. We can shift our vibrations, in the form of thoughts, to those that are more harmonious with our desires, and we can then begin to take the small steps necessary for our inspiration to be sensed. Source energy will cooperate with us when we seek it energetically—moreover, we can begin to reassess our lives for misaligned attractions and imagined bad luck.

With a mental shift of this nature, someone could question why he'd elect to come here as a homosexual, when all it's done is bring him trouble: Parents rejected him, he was the recipient of ridicule throughout childhood, employment opportunities eluded him, and he faced discrimination in every area of his life. Well, maybe if he looks deeper into his spiritual origins, he'd discover that he signed up to teach others to love and accept those who aren't in the mainstream of life. What better way to do so than to have a life in a body that's so easily stereotyped? If this felt true, that person would recognize his calling to be involved in changing prejudicial reactions. Regardless of what goes on in the world of form, inside himself he'd be living in-Spirit.

When we feel peaceful within, we begin to attract more of the peace we desire because we're functioning from a spiritual place of peace. When we engage Spirit, we regain the power of our ultimate Source. Likewise, a beggar on a street corner may have agreed to come into this world of boundaries to teach and generate the awareness that leads to more compassion in this world—or even to teach a single person (perhaps you) to be more compassionate. After all, Source shows up in an endless array of costumes. . . .

In an infinite Universe, there's no time restriction on how many lifetimes we get. With an infinity before us, spending one lifetime teaching compassion doesn't seem outrageous. Similarly, the autistic child, the blind person, the victim of violence, the aborted fetus, the quadriplegic, the starving child, and you—with whatever infirmities and difficulties you've attracted—are part of the perfection of this Universe. The desire to change and improve our world is also a part of that perfection. Therefore, an inspirational attitude is less judgmental and more appreciative, with a keen eye for how God, or Source energy, manifests. And remember: *Source can't be removed from what It creates.*

I love this story that Sri Swami Satchidananda tells in his wonderful book *Beyond Words.* I had the great pleasure of meeting with Swami on several occasions, and he was a supremely inspired being right up until his transition back to nonphysical spirit a few years ago.

> There was a man a long time ago who prayed every day, "God, I really want You to come in person, to have a nice sumptuous lunch with me."
>
> Because he was constantly nagging, God appeared one day and said, "Okay, I'll come."
>
> "God, I'm so happy. When can You come? You must give me some time to prepare everything."
>
> "Okay, I'll come on Friday."
>
> Before He left, the man asked, "Can I invite my friends?"
>
> "Sure," God said. And then He disappeared.

The man invited everybody and started preparing all kinds of delicious food. Friday at noon a huge dining table was set up. Everybody was there, with a big garland and water to wash God's feet. The man knew that God is punctual. When he heard the clock chiming twelve, he said, "What happened? God wouldn't disappoint me. He can't be late. Human beings can be late, but not God."

He was a little puzzled but decided to wait another half hour as a courtesy. Still no God. Then the guests began speaking, "You fool, you said God was coming. We had doubts. Why on Earth would God come and eat with you? Come, let's go."

The man said, "No, wait," and walked inside to see what was happening.

To his great anxiety, he saw a big black dog on the dining table, eating everything there. "Oh, no! God sensed that the lunch was already eaten by a dog. That's why he didn't want to come." He took a big club and started beating the dog. The dog cried and ran away.

Then the man came out to his guests and said, "What can I do? Now, neither God nor you can eat because the food was polluted by a dog. I know that's why God didn't come." He felt so bad that he went back and started praying. Finally God appeared to him again, but there were wounds and bandages all over his body.

"What happened?" asked the man. "You must have gotten into a terrible accident."

"It was no accident," said God. "It was you!"

"Why do You blame me?"

"Because I came punctually at noon and started eating. Then you came and beat Me. You clubbed Me and broke My bones."

"But You didn't come!"

"Are you sure nobody was eating your food?"

"Well, yes, there was a black dog."

"Who is that, then, if not Me? I really wanted to enjoy your food, so I came as a dog."

Everyone and everything contains God or the Source, so be on the lookout for the God-force in every living thing. Explore how this force has delivered to us many blessings in disguise.

We came from a world of pure Spirit and allowed that Source

to take over without any interference or questioning on our part. As long as we were in-Spirit, our Source materialized in a multitude of ways to handle everything. Then, almost immediately after our birth into form, we initiated a program to deny Spirit and emphasize the ego.

But now, as you read these words, you're on the threshold of dropping ego identity and returning to a life where inspiration awaits you. Here are some suggestions to assist you in crossing that threshold.

Some Suggestions for Putting the Ideas in This Chapter to Work for You

— See yourself as a single cell in a body called humanity, and vow to be a cell that cooperates with all adjacent cells with a sense of belonging to the whole. View uninspired thoughts and actions as impinging on your well-being *and* that of all humanity.

— Make a concerted effort to allow the natural-healing and well-being capacity of your body to play itself out. Refuse to focus on what's wrong in your body and in your life; rather, shift your thoughts to those that allow you to stay in harmony with your Source energy. For example, rather than saying, "I feel sick [or tired]," say, "I want to feel good, so I'll allow my natural connection to well-being to take over right now." Your reformed self-talk invites the flow of inspiration.

— Inventory all the people who were negative and/or destructive elements in your past, and search for ways that their actions might have been helpful events and attitudes that were just disguised as impediments to happiness. For example, my stepfather's alcoholism and drunken ways, which I despised at the time, were powerfully instrumental in helping me deal with my own addictions later on in life. Abandonment, abuse, and disloyalty can be painfully difficult and valuable teachers when you see yourself as having experienced them for a greater good.

— Imagine a conversation, just before your conception, with the Creative Spirit that you materialized from. Review the parents and siblings you selected, as well as the timing of your birth. Find ways that those participants in your life were aligned with the deep inner urge you had as an exclusively spiritual entity to accomplish a calling. Try to make sense of what may at first appear to be a jumble of unrelated items in your life. If this exercise satisfies and inspires you, there's no need to convince anyone else.

— Be mindful of the perfection of the Universe and the Creative Source behind it by noticing whenever you bang your elbow, stub your toe, get hit by a falling tree branch, and so forth. When such events happen, stop and ask yourself, "What was I thinking in that precise moment, and how is it related to what appeared to be an accident?" You'll discover a pattern: What you're thinking is usually mysteriously tied in with what's taking place from moment to moment. Do this to create a constant awareness of your Source and the direction of your life.

* * *

In the next chapter, we'll explore why we left the world where we were in-Spirit. Keep in mind the ancient simple truth that *the mighty oak was once a little nut that held its ground.* We're all a mighty oak in the making, and it's all right to be a little nutty as long as we also hold our ground!

CHAPTER 3

WHY WE LEFT OUR FULL-TIME SPIRITUAL IDENTITY BEHIND

*"A sense of separation from God
is the only lack you really need correct."*

— FROM *A COURSE IN MIRACLES*

WE NOW UNDERSTAND that we were created out of Spirit, so It must be a part of us. We also realize that for nine months, we totally trusted in this originating Spirit, and all we needed was provided for—and then we arrived as a pure representation of Spirit. So why did most of us trade in the "spiritual identity card" for one that wants us to believe in things that are nonexistent where we came from, such as suffering, fear, anxiety, limits, and worries? The answer lies in understanding why we left behind our full-time participation in the world of Spirit.

I've used the term *full-time* to signify that we're always connected to Spirit, even when we think and behave in ways that don't reflect spiritual consciousness. What I'm offering in this book is the awareness that we can return to a full-time position of inspiration, which is the true meaning of our life.

Inspiration can be cultivated and be a driving enthusiasm

throughout life, rather than showing up every now and then and just as mysteriously disappearing, seemingly independent of our desire. And it's *everyone's* Divine birthright—that is, it isn't reserved for high-profile creative geniuses in the arts and sciences. The problem is that from birth we're gradually taught to believe exclusively in the world ruled by Club Ego . . . and we put our full-time membership in Club Spirit on hold.

Our Initiation into Club Ego

When we arrive in this physical world, we're immediately cared for by well-meaning folks who've been taught to believe in the illusion of what Patanjali called "the false self." They think that they're not defined by the spiritual essence from which they came, but by their uniquely special individuality, their possessions, and their accomplishments. They see themselves as separate from each other, from what's materially missing in their lives, and from God.

You can see why the word *ego* is often referred to as an acronym for **e**dging **G**od **o**ut. Ego, you see, is an idea that we acquire from our clogged environment, which is stuffed full of ego-dominated folks. I'm not using the word *ego* to describe overly self-important people who thrive on nauseating delusions of grandeur; rather, I mean it as a catch-all term for defining identification with the false self.

Very early on, ego tells us that we're separate from everyone else—directly contradicting Spirit, which reminds us that we share the same life force with everyone. Ego nags us to compete and insists that we've failed when others defeat us or have more than we do. And more than anything else, ego fears our living an inspired life because then we'll have no need for it.

As we progressed through our developmental years, we weren't trained to stay in-Spirit—quite the opposite! We were constantly reminded that we were what we did in life, and failure to accomplish the kind of life that others saw for us meant that we should feel dejected. Our culture wanted us to learn early that we are what we acquire, and if we have or want very little, then *we* are of very little value. Furthermore, we are what others think of us, so if our reputation is sullied, we're of even less value!

We were indoctrinated in these lessons by family, church, community, school, the media, and even strangers. These ego-dominated edicts were force-fed to us and allowed to mute the deep inner voice that beckoned us to remember why we're here. Eventually, we learned to ignore those in-Spirit murmurs and replace joy, contentment, and bliss with an emptiness that wonders, *What's it all about?* We opted to fit in, chasing someone else's dream and counting up our earnings and possessions to measure our level of success. The nagging feeling that resulted is the result of relinquishing our true spiritual self as an active participant in this life. But take heart: It never left us, and is alive within us today.

Ego's Dominating Messages

We can start returning to being in-Spirit by examining what ego has accomplished in our life, as well as making a determined effort to resist the powerful pressures of *our culture's* ego in favor of an inspired life. Ego is just an illusion . . . so ask yourself if you wish to continue to be controlled by something that isn't true, or would you rather look into what's real and never changes? Keep in mind that Spirit is fixed, permanent, and infinite, while ego comes and goes with the wind.

To continue on with this discussion, I've adapted the following list from a fascinating book called *The Disappearance of the Universe* (Hay House, 2004) by Gary Renard, which gives an account of two spiritual visitors teaching Gary the significance of *A Course in Miracles.* Whether you accept the premise or not is your option—*I* find these teachings to be profound, and they merit consideration.

1. The ego says, "You're a body." The Holy Spirit says, "You're not even a person—you're just like Me, your Source of being." This teaching shows that our ego insists we're impermanent, which is opposed to our being what Lao-tzu (the mystical spiritual teacher of the 6th century B.C.) taught: that which never changes. When we think about our life here on Earth, we can't avoid the awareness that everything we experience, including our body, returns to dust to be recycled by Spirit. Our ego finds this concept impossible to accept.

2. The ego says, "Your thoughts are very important." The Holy Spirit insists, "Only thoughts you think with God are real—nothing else matters." This teaching explains that thoughts centering on ourselves, appearance, possessions, fears, or relationship problems are not only unimportant, they're not real. *Ouch!* The ego flinches at such commentary. But if we examine these thoughts from Spirit's infinite perspective, we see that they're indeed unreal. When we were totally immersed in-Spirit, we only had thoughts of Spirit because that's all we were; when we left It behind, we opted for thoughts that our ego told us were important. *A Course in Miracles* tells us that we didn't even have to think in heaven because we were thought by God. So we can access permanent inspiration by letting ourselves once again be thought by God and achieve a state of heaven on Earth.

3. Your ego says, "The Lord giveth and the Lord taketh away." The Holy Spirit asserts, "God only gives and never takes away." When living an inspired life, we're focused on giving our life away and simultaneously observing how it's returned, thus fortifying the idea of what goes around comes around. Ego is constantly telling us to be fearful about losing what we have and warning us of greedy others who'll take what's ours—but God doesn't take away from us. As we learn to think this way, we attract more of what's missing in our life. The reason for this is simple: We become what we think about. If we think about giving, like God does, the

Universe will provide. If we think about things being taken away, then that's what we'll attract.

4. The ego says, "There's good and bad." The Holy Spirit maintains, "There's nothing to judge because it isn't real in the first place." When we accept the ego identification card, we agree to judge almost everyone and everything in terms of good or bad. The problem with this is that we *all* contain the same Spirit from which we originated. If I make you bad and myself good, for instance, I deny the presence of Spirit in you whom I elected to judge. God sees it quite differently: Our spiritual Source knows that *only It is real*—all of the ephemeral world of form and boundaries is not of Its infinite nature. At our core, the place where we all originate from and return to, there's no one and nothing to judge. This takes some time to get used to, but once we grasp the truth of this observation, we're free to tap in to authentic inspiration.

5. The ego directs love and hate toward individuals. The Holy Spirit's love is nonspecific and all-encompassing. Ego directs us to love some, be indifferent toward many, and hate all others. When we learn to be back in-Spirit on a full-time basis, we discover what we knew in our pre-ego time: There's no "they," there's only "one." The one Source of all-encompassing love knows nothing of boundaries; differing customs; geographic divisions; family splits; or differences in race, creed, sex, and so on—It only knows *love for all.*

Ego is probably working on you right now as you read, attempting to convince you of the folly of such thinking. It may retort, "How can you love those who would harm you and are your declared enemies?" When your ego speaks in this way, recall the words of Jesus: "You have heard that it was said 'love your neighbor and hate your enemy'" (Matt. 5:43). This is how ego works—it tells you to divide your love for some and offer your hate to others. Yet Jesus, who lived totally in-Spirit, goes on to say, "But I tell you: love your enemies and pray for those who persecute you, that you may be sons of your Father in heaven" (Matt. 5:44–45).

Jesus points so perfectly to the differences between ego and Spirit. When we were in-Spirit, we were a child of our Father in heaven and "He causes his sun to rise on the evil and the good" (Matt. 5:45). This, of course, means that it's all one: Evil, good, righteous, and unrighteous are all the same—some move away from the Father, some move toward Him. This is such an important and powerful lesson to get as we move toward becoming inspired by living in-Spirit.

6. The ego devises clever reasons why we should continue to listen to its selfish counsel. The Holy Spirit is certain that at some point we'll turn toward It and ultimately return. Ego will tout its irresistible logic to assure us that our body, our possessions, and our achievements are all very real and important. It convinces us by insisting that what's real is what we can see, touch, hear, taste, and smell; therefore, invisible Spirit isn't real. So ego continues to be attached to stuff and to make the acquisition of money and power a life-long objective. To that end, it wants us to disdain forgiveness in favor of seeking revenge—very persuasive logic when we look around and see almost everyone doing just that.

Through the lens of inspiration, however, we're able to see how ego has distorted the message of the Holy Spirit—instead of seeking revenge, we're more likely to see a very sad nation of strivers and virtually no arrivers; a gaggle of pill poppers, searching outside of themselves for a resolution to their depressing, anxiety-filled, joy-less, and often lonely lives. As we return to the Holy Spirit, we'll no longer be under the influence of ego's absurd counsel.

7. The ego wants us to regret our past. The Holy Spirit wants us to practice unconditional forgiveness. The Holy Spirit isn't limited by a past or a future—there's only the eternal now. Any energy we place on what transpired in the past is ground-work for guilt, and ego *loves* guilt. Such negative energy fabricates an excuse for why our present moments are troubled and gives us a cop-out, a reason to stay out of Spirit. And thinking about where we've been or what we did wrong in the past are great impediments to an inspired life.

On the other hand, when we're inspired, we're totally engaged in the now. In an infinite never-beginning and never-ending Universe, there can be no past. All guilt and regret simply serve as ways to avoid being here in the only moment we have, which is now. This is where we reconnect to Spirit—*now*. If we choose to use up this holy instant with regrets about a past that's only an illusory thought, then we're unable to be in the joyful, loving, peaceful, present moment. Cramming this holy moment with thoughts of guilt, remorse, and regret is great for ego . . . and keeps us totally resistant to being in-Spirit.

These seven messages are the dominant ones the ego drones on about. If we don't listen, it will try to drown out inspiration by intensifying worrisome and fearful thoughts. I've managed to tame this annoying voice of the ego so that its influence is almost negligible in my life, and I know you can, too.

How I Learned to Slay the Ego Intruder

I realize that the ego's voice has most of us convinced that we're powerless to manage our own destiny. There was a time when I felt much more kindly toward the ego, since it plays such a dominant role in the lives of so many people—but today I see it as something that needs to be destroyed. I no longer agree that since it's in our lives, we might just as well learn to love and accept it, troublesome as it might be; nor do I believe that it serves some useful purpose. Knowing that we've been created in the image of our Creator, and therefore have the same essence *and* the same ultimate potential, means that ego is out of the picture! Ego denies our original invisible reality, so it must be removed and completely banished from our awareness.

Realizing that ego is a traitor to our greatness is what ultimately set me free of its pull. I keep remembering that ego isn't real, even as it still protests and attempts to delete my feelings of inspiration. My highest self responds with, "But remember, Wayne, what's trying to drag you down isn't real."

What also helps to keep me on track is parenting. I'm the father of eight children, so I can recall thousands of instances of being sucked into a black hole of confusion and uncertainty with my kids. Arguments with them concerning schoolwork, questionable friendships, curfews, staying at a pal's house, dress codes, dating, cigarettes or drugs, what was right from my perspective and wrong from theirs (and vice versa) . . . on and on this list could go. There were anger and hurt feelings, sleepless nights, and of course, much happiness, joy, and contentment, too.

As I look back on those years of parent/child conflicts, I realize today, in this now moment, that none of it exists. It isn't real because it's in the changing world of time and space. Similarly, I now realize that every conflict or struggle that exists, as well as those experiences I'd call good and joyful, are not real from the inspirational point of view. So if anything I experience is immediately going to fall into illusion, why not simply stay connected to Spirit through it all?

While I still have occasions when I slip, today I'm able to say that every conflict I have with my mostly now-adult children (or anyone else for that matter) isn't really between me and them—it's between me and God. I look for a way to be like God and stay loving, caring, forgiving, and peaceful within myself, suspending my need to be right and knowing that in the next moment it will all be gone . . . which is true of everything that's being played out in this illusory world.

I want to emphasize that I'm not suggesting that peace means being in a place where there's no noise or trouble; rather, it means that in the *midst* of turmoil, I can still feel calm. Not one of the things that I was so upset and out of control over matters today— not one. It's all illusion fed by my ego's need to make me important by "winning," "being right," or "coming out on top."

* * *

I'll conclude this chapter a little differently by presenting a few passages from the Bhagavad Gita, the holy book of the Hindus, on which Mahatma Gandhi based his life. These passages speak to our leaving that world of pure Spirit and inspiration and incarnating into a body and reflect, in ancient spiritual verse, what I've attempted to convey. (Notice in this highly respected spiritual text that the word *Self* is capitalized—this is to signify the spiritual, eternal Self.)

The Self dwells in the house of the body,
Which passes through childhood, youth, and old age.
So passes the Self at the time of death
Into another body. The wise know this truth
And are not deceived by it.

When the senses come in contact with sense-objects
They give rise to feelings of heat and cold,
Pleasure and pain, which come and go.
Accept them calmly, as do the wise.

The wise, who live free from pleasure and pain,
Are worthy of immortality.

As I've tried to express in this chapter, pleasure and pain and troubles and good times aren't eternal—Krishna advises us to accept them calmly, but stay detached. If we do, we'll live in-Spirit in what I call immortality.

Not pierced by arrows nor burnt by fire,
Affected by neither water nor wind,
The Self is not a physical creature.

Not wounded, not burnt, not wetted, not dried,
The Self is ever and everywhere,
Immovable and everlasting.

This spiritual classic reminds us that we're not only physical creatures with egos—we're a Self to which we wish to be wedded in-Spirit, which is everywhere and everlasting. This is our true essence. When we move into this space within ourselves and see all of our life experiences from this point of view, we'll be permanently inspired.

Some there are who have realized the Self
In all its wonder. Others can speak of it
As wonderful. But there are many
Who don't understand even when they hear.

Deathless is the Self in every creature.
Know this truth, and leave all sorrow behind.

When we do as Krishna advises and realize the Self, we live knowing that our true being is deathless. This is a great comfort, as we can leave sorrow behind and be inspired.

Some Suggestions for Putting the Ideas in This Chapter to Work for You

— Seeing this physical world as an illusion ironically allows you to enjoy it more and stay inspired. Practice laughing at the importance that you and so many people place on everyday circumstances. View it from an eternal perspective, and you'll find yourself lightening that heavy load. (I've personally often cited the words *this too shall pass* to keep me unburdened when my imagined problems feel troublesome.)

Your ego wants you to live in a state of self-importance, but your Holy Spirit knows that the only thing that's truly important is being in alignment with Spirit. Therefore, anything that's not of Spirit—such as fear, illness, worry, shame, anger, and the like—is worthy of your laughter.

— When others attempt to seduce you into feeling bad, guilty, worried, fearful, or anything that isn't of Spirit, practice stepping outside of yourself and becoming the observer to all things transitory, which is your entire physical world. Repeat sentiments such as "This isn't mine," "I refuse to own it," and "I'll not be misaligned with Spirit." At any moment of your life, you can practice this observer technique: Just mentally step outside of your body and observe what's trying to keep you from being inspired. Then vow to return to Spirit by repeating the above statements.

— Continually remind yourself of the physical and metaphysical truth that there's no place anywhere in this Universe that's devoid of Spirit. Everything and everyone is of Spirit before, during, and after manifestation into physical form. I urge you to seek this Spirit when your ego has convinced you that It's absent. In all of your noninspired moments, practice stopping the chatter of the ego and look for the good, or a reason for what's happening. Even in devastating natural disasters such as hurricanes, tsunamis, floods, fires, and the like, look for the good. There's no death from the perspective of infinity, so once you've removed the horror of dying from the equation, you'll have a different perspective.

— The lost lives of others teach us all to be more in-Spirit: to be kinder, to grow in caring and compassion, creating an increased sensitivity to the oneness in the Universe. We can translate these heightened sensitivities into behavior that's more giving and forgiving, extending assistance and cooperating with each other. You'll discover a way of following your own instincts to be more in-Spirit and less in fear and anger.

— Die while you're alive. Live the words of the New Testament that tell you that you're *in* this world but not *of* it. You can be here without being attached to here by simply discarding your body identification: Imagine yourself as a decomposed energy field that's impervious to anything not of Spirit. Envision, for example, that criticism and feelings of inadequacy are *in* this world and thus unable to enter your body because you've left it and are a translucent glob of nonparticles that's no longer *of* this world.

This exercise will liberate you from so many of the problems you've connected to in your mind. You only have now, and even it will disappear in a flash. Welcome to the infinite world of Spirit! As H. L. Mencken, a famous journalist/satirist of a generation ago, wrote: "We are here and it is now: further than that, all human knowledge is moonshine."

— Work every day to tame ego's demands. Ultimately, make it your goal to unashamedly slay your ego while you're still in your body—it's doomed to destruction at the moment you die and re-enter the realm of reality from which you came anyway. Keep in mind that you're not being cruel by destroying your ego, since it's a false self to begin with.

✳ ✳ ✳

The best way I can think of to summarize and conclude this chapter is to take you back to the opening quotation from *A Course in Miracles*. To me, this observation helps us understand why we've left our spiritual identification: "A sense of separation from God is the only lack you really need correct."

Now let's work on correcting that separation.

CHAPTER 4

HOW IT FEELS TO RETURN TO SPIRIT

"The aim and purpose of human life
is the unitive knowledge of God."

— ALDOUS HUXLEY

THIS MUCH SHOULD BE CLEAR BY NOW: We originated in a field of energy that has no boundaries. Before entering the world of form, we were in-Spirit—a piece of God, if you will. We began entering this physical world first as a particle, then as a cell, then as a fetus, then as an infant, and ultimately as a fully developed human being. But our ultimate purpose all along was to experience "the unitive knowledge of God," as Huxley so beautifully puts it.

Sadly, when we began our human training, we were taught to abandon most of our spiritual identity and adopt a new one based on ego consciousness, or a sense of being separate from Spirit. In other words, we came here from a place of inspiration and intended to stay that way—unfortunately, we forgot to do so, and we ended up abandoning most of our inspiring notions in favor of a consensus of "reality" that didn't include Spirit. We chose the false self, which is why we so inexplicably feel off-purpose.

In the West, traditional psychology hasn't wholeheartedly embraced the existence of Atman, the godhead within humans, and our psychological and spiritual teachings don't show us how to achieve the union of perfect yoga. (For this kind of learning, we'd have to study with a teacher of yoga or organized religion.) Now we'd like to reconnect to the world of Spirit, while at the same time not shed the familiar body we've worn for a lifetime. That's where Patanjali's teachings come in.

Patanjali was considered a saint in his lifetime, teaching *sutras* (the essential threads of a philosophy) that elevated human beings to their highest potential. He taught about knowing God through the practice of meditation and yoga in order to attain a point of union with the Source. He also described our ability to perform miracles—these feats involved specific spiritual aphorisms and the daily practice of yoga. The remainder of this chapter is devoted to my impression of Patanjali's 2,300-year-old observations on inspiration.

When You Are Inspired . . .

My personal view of the six ideas presented here includes my belief in the existence of a God-consciousness within every one of us. And my purpose in the next few pages is to help you achieve this perfect union of yoga and live from this inspired perspective every day.

Here's what Patanjali offered us more than 2,000 years ago, which is the most profound statement I've ever found on the significance of the role of our ultimate calling:

> When you are inspired by some great purpose, some extraordinary project, all your thoughts break their bonds, your mind transcends limitations, your consciousness expands in every direction, and you find yourself in a new, great, and wonderful world. Dormant forces, faculties, and talents become alive, and you discover yourself to be a greater person by far than you ever dreamed yourself to be.

Patanjali opens his aphorism with an observation on inspiration and follows it up with six conclusions. These six key points are the basis for this chapter, as they describe what it feels like when we return to the world of Spirit.

1. When You Are Inspired . . .
All Your Thoughts Break Their Bonds

As I explained earlier, being inspired is equivalent to being back in-Spirit. Before we showed up in form, our mind and the mind of God were synonymous, which means that we were free from the bonds of the ego mind. This is simply how the world of Spirit works: It's impossible to have limiting boundaries or self-imposed shackles placed on us. When we're in harmony with the mind of God, we simply don't have thoughts that tell us we can't accomplish something—after all, our thoughts are of a higher energy.

Every desire we have has an energy-vibration component to it. When we launch that desire in the form of a thought, it generally matches up with the same energy vibration of our spiritual Source: *I want to attract prosperity, I want to experience physical well-being, I want to have a peaceful relationship, I want to feel good about my life,* and so on. The energy of our thoughts determines whether or not we're living at an inspired level, so any doubt in our ability to manifest our desire or to receive spiritual guidance is vibrationally out of tune with that desire. And when this occurs, we automatically impose bonds on our mind—which most frequently assume the form of thoughts that imperil our ability to be inspired.

Returning to Spirit results in a grand sense of being in tune with our uniquely Divine purpose. Just imagine being able to go on and on for hours at a time without experiencing fatigue, hunger, thirst, or mental exhaustion, all thanks to one factor: the willingness to be back in-Spirit. I've personally found that when I have thoughts of being "inspired by some great purpose [or] extraordinary project," I let go of fatigue; that is, being in-Spirit somehow eliminates thoughts that send the "I'm exhausted" signals to my body. In the middle of writing, speaking, touring with my family, playing a tennis match, or anything that inspires me, all bonds are shattered by my mind, and fatigue is impossible.

Furthermore, matching up my desires with plans and behavior in the form of my thoughts and actions breaks down the bonds of hunger and discomfort. I've literally written for up to 14 hours without eating or experiencing any hunger pangs. Somehow being inspired allows my thoughts to remove any of the bonds that can serve as excuses not to do what I know I'm here to accomplish.

This observation that Patanjali made so long ago is awesome. Why not practice returning to Spirit and allowing all thoughts to be in agreement with that originating Spirit? Your thoughts will work on your body and surroundings, transforming obstacles into the fulfillment of desires.

2. When You Are Inspired . . .
Your Mind Transcends Limitations

Next, imagine what it must feel like to have absolute faith—an inner knowing that it's impossible to fail, a complete absence of doubt concerning your ability to create anything you place your attention on. I imagine that must be how God feels when preparing to create—He must have this kind of confidence about the outcome.

Well, when we're inspired, we remember that God is always in us and we're always in God, so we're incapable of thinking limited thoughts. We're transcendent; we've gone beyond the world of boundaries and entered a space of creative knowing. In other words, we surrender . . . we put ourselves under the guidance and control of our Purposeful Force.

I can personally vouch for this surrendering process. During my life I've had an unshakable faith in my ability to attract money and prosperity—even as a youngster living in foster homes, I always felt I was entitled to have wealth. I just *knew* there was an inexhaustible supply and that it was totally neutral, simply an energy that goes wherever it's called to go. I don't know why I've known this my entire life, but I know it even more today.

A television interviewer once asked me if I ever felt guilty about making so much from my writings and recordings. I responded, much to her surprise, "I would feel guilty, except that it's not my fault." When she asked what I meant, I explained that money has always come to me because I've always felt within me that I *am* money. I attract prosperity because I feel entitled to it; in fact, I feel that it's actually a definition of me. Money has always come to me, and because it has, I direct *it* wherever I perceive it to be needed. It's simply an energy system that my mind has created—it flows to me because it's who I am. I've never doubted that I came from an energy field of pure unlimited abundance, and because of my unshakable faith, I've always acted on this prosperity consciousness. I've never known a moment of unemployment, through good or bad economic times.

When I was a little kid, I saw that collecting soda-pop bottles would bring in pennies and that pennies became dollars. I saw that helping ladies with their groceries, shoveling their snow, or emptying their ashes from the coal furnaces were acts of prosperity. And today, I'm still collecting pop bottles, shoveling snow, and carrying out ashes on a much larger scale. Prosperity continues to chase after me because I'm still in total harmony with my originating Spirit, which is abundance and prosperity.

A few months back, the NFL's rushing champion of 2004, Curtis Martin of the New York Jets, was in the front row of a lecture I presented at Westbury Music Fair on Long Island. At the conclusion of the evening, this gentleman—who's reached the pinnacle in his own profession—came up to me and pressed a piece of paper into my hand as he thanked me for the lecture.

Back in my hotel room, I realized that Mr. Martin had given me a personal check for $5,000, with no restrictions or instructions. You see, as I told the interviewer, it's not my fault! (I matched the gift that Curtis gave to me and contributed it toward a van for a woman on Maui who's been in a wheelchair for more than 22 years.) Indeed, when we're inspired, we attract the abundance from that which we originated. And the mind then truly transcends every limitation.

3. When You Are Inspired . . .
Your Consciousness Expands in Every Direction

Now try to imagine yourself living in a world that has no direction: There's no north, south, east, or west; there's no up or down; and there's no past or future. In this world, *any* direction is *every* direction. As difficult as it is to imagine a directionless Universe, that's exactly what the world of Spirit looks and feels like.

When we're in-Spirit, every direction is possible for us at every moment because our consciousness happens within our mind. Now this inner world of ours, reunited with its originating essence, doesn't think in only one direction; rather, it allows all possibilities. Our consciousness is in the absolute state of allowing—all resistance, in the form of thoughts, is nonexistent.

I'm speaking of a feeling that comes over us when we're inspired by a "great purpose, [an] extraordinary project," where we experience the bliss of an expanded consciousness with the unsurpassed allowing of any and all possibilities to enter into our daily life. We cease looking for answers in a directional way—they don't come from someplace north or west of us, nor are they arriving from up above or impeded by something down below. We begin to feel the larger sense of life, what being a part of *all* is like once again.

Is there any place that God isn't? And if we came from God, then mustn't we be like God? You see, we're already connected to everything we need when we're inspired—what takes place is a realignment within us that allows for every thing, every event, and every person to merge in our inspirited consciousness. When we reemerge into the perfect oneness of Spirit, we view everyone we meet as an ally through our inspired way of life. We feel extraordinarily guided and attract people, events, and circumstances to join us in our inspired state because our world has transcended from the elementary cause-and-effect, birth-to-death path to all directions simultaneously. We're living at maximum *allowing*, with nonexistent resistance. We're back in-Spirit.

4. When You Are Inspired . . .
You Find Yourself in a New, Great, and Wonderful World

Patanjali was so right with this conclusion—we absolutely enter into a new world when we become inspired. We feel different because we're no longer edging God out. We're back in vibrational alignment where limitations don't exist and there are no bonds, and we've left our body and all of its boundaries to live in an expanded consciousness in our mind. We now begin to think in terms of miracles being not only possible, but actively en route. Soon we stop being surprised by all the things that are going our way and instead affirm: *What is needed is on its way.* The phrase *We expect miracles* is more than a New Age slogan, it's how we feel when we live each day in-Spirit. We leave the world of anxiety, fear, doubt, and impossibility and enter a new, wonderful world of Spirit, where all things are possible.

In 1976, I made the choice to live in-Spirit on a full-time basis. I resigned from my professorship at St. John's University to teach and write on a much larger stage. I knew within myself that I was finally listening in earnest to the inner voice that chose my destiny before I was conceived. I incarnated to teach self-reliance and to help our planet move to a more unified means of living in heaven on Earth, but I was here for 35 years before devoting myself exclusively to my mission.

At the age of 36, I was consumed by my writing and by telling the world about my book *Your Erroneous Zones*—I was filled with excitement and passion about what I was involved in. I had never felt as complete in my previous 35 years, even though I had an exciting and thoroughly satisfying career teaching and counseling. The moment I resigned from being an employee to living my dream—when I mustered up the courage to be in-Spirit—lives in my mind even today, some 30 years later. What happened from that moment on is precisely what Patanjali suggests. I found myself in a "new, great, and wonderful world." It was as if a huge blanket had been removed from me, and breezes were allowed to refresh me at every turn I made. The world became my oyster when I shifted into the world of inspiration.

Suddenly I began receiving requests to appear on radio and TV shows to discuss what I believed in so passionately. The more I spoke (from what I now recognize as inspiration), the more invitations I received. Radio hosts began asking me to fill in—sometimes for six or seven hours on all-night shows, and then for a week at a time—in cities across the country. I stayed with my inspiration, loving every moment, working 18-hour days, and being willing to do whatever it took to stay in-Spirit.

Soon national shows took an interest in me, and all the while, precisely the right people showed up to teach and guide me through this process. Publicists, editors, book distributors, talent coordinators, travel agents, bankers . . . everyone who was needed kept surfacing. All I had to do was stay inspired, and "follow [my] bliss," in the words of Joseph Campbell—it was as if a gigantic hand was pulling the right strings. Moment by moment, day by day, I was in awe of it all at the time, and I'm still in awe as I write these words many years later. Today, more than ever, I trust in Patanjali's advice to stay in-Spirit.

This is not to say that many obstacles didn't surface, as they continue to today. There are times when I still can't fathom why I have to go through so many difficulties. At the age of 65 I thought I was through with heartbreak, yet I still have it coming at me. A debilitating heart attack, a personal tragedy in my private life, and serious addiction challenges within my family have all been recent occurrences. Despite all the hardships that have surfaced, I've found that all these experiences are valuable because of the compassion, forgiveness, and kindness that I've developed.

These so-called negative situations have impacted my writing and speaking and have caused me to reach out to a much larger audience through public television, where I offer a positive, inspired message. My lesson has been to stay in-Spirit and step outside my body and my life circumstances to observe all that has and continues to flow to me from a perspective of detachment. It's not about me; it's about staying in-Spirit, knowing that all that comes my way is a Divine blessing—even the struggles.

Here's a tale about ways of dealing with adversity that I find particularly thought provoking and inspiring:

Carrots, Eggs, and Coffee

A young woman complained to her mother about the hardships and difficulties in her life. She didn't know how she was going to continue and wanted to give up. The young woman said, "I'm tired of fighting and struggling. It seems that as soon as one problem is solved, a new one appears." In response, her mother took her to the kitchen and filled three pots with water, placing each on the stove over a high flame.

Soon the water came to boil. In the first pot she placed carrots, in the second she placed eggs, and in the last she placed ground coffee beans. She let them sit and boil, without saying a word. In about 20 minutes, she turned off the burners. The mother then fished the carrots out and placed them in a bowl. She removed the eggs and placed them in a bowl. Then she ladled the coffee out and placed it in a bowl. Turning to her daughter, she said, "Tell me what you see."

"Carrots, eggs, and coffee," the daughter replied. Her mother brought her closer and asked her to feel the carrots. She did and noted that they were soft. The mother then asked the daughter to take an egg and break it. After peeling off the shell, she observed the hard-boiled egg. Finally, the mother asked the daughter to sip the coffee. The daughter smiled as she tasted its rich flavor.

The daughter then asked, "What does it mean, Mother?"

Her mother explained that each of these objects had faced the same adversity, boiling water, and each reacted differently. The carrot went in strong, hard, and unrelenting. However, after being subjected to the boiling water, it softened and became weak. The egg had been fragile, its thin outer shell protecting its liquid interior, but after the boiling water, its inside became hardened. But the ground coffee beans were unique—after they were in the boiling water, they'd changed the water itself.

The message? Stay in-Spirit and change adversity into a component of a new, great, and wonderful world, just as the coffee did.

5. When You Are Inspired . . .
Dormant Forces, Faculties, and Talents Become Alive

I love Patanjali for teaching me this powerful truth. Essentially, he's telling us that when we move into an awareness of inspiration, forces that we thought were either dead or unavailable come alive and are available for us to use to manifest our inspired desires. Could this be true? Does the Universe collaborate with us in awakening long-slumbering forces, faculties, and talents? I know it to be true, so my answer is an unqualified *yes!* I use this particular insight every day of my life—in fact, I'm using it in this very moment.

I'm confident that what I'm supposed to say in these pages will come to me in one form or another, especially since I live and breathe this idea of inspiration—I'm so passionate about helping others learn how important it is to hear *their* ultimate calling. I sleep with a pad of paper and a pen next to my bed because much of what I wish to convey comes via my dream state. As I walk along the beach here on Maui, watching the humpback whales and dolphins dancing offshore, I ask them for guidance. I receive it, note it, and share it with you.

I know that forces exist to guide me through every stage of this writing. When I pick up a book, I often open it to precisely the right page, and exactly what I need appears before me. I smile inwardly and say aloud, "Thank you, God. You're always there for me when I write, seemingly alone here in my dining room and looking out at the magnificent ocean."

I love watching those dormant forces come alive and guide me in my own inspired offerings. I so appreciate the talent that's rested within me for so long awakening when I do what I know I'm here to do. I certainly couldn't access the forces if I were living at the ordinary level of consciousness that had been laid out for me by external well-meaning forces. I can only access the dormant forces when I'm inspired—that is, when I let go of my ego demands and reenter that magical realm of Spirit.

These dormant forces will come to all of us—they're actually alive and well and have been working on our behalf for as long as we've been here. Yet they appear to be dead to us because we've left behind our Divine purpose, which we decided on long before we took on the insane ego.

I've always loved great stories of synchronicity. Here's one (considered to be an urban legend by some) that illustrates how the Universe conspires to guide those who opt for a life of inspiration:

A poor Scottish farmer named Fleming heard a cry for help coming from a nearby bog. He dropped his tools and ran to it. There, mired up to his waist in black muck, was a terrified boy, screaming and trying to free himself. Farmer Fleming saved the child from what could have been a slow and horrible death. On the following day, a fancy carriage pulled up to the Scotsman's sparse surroundings. An elegantly dressed nobleman stepped out and introduced himself as the father of the boy Farmer Fleming had saved. "I want to repay you," said the nobleman. "You saved my son's life."

"No, I can't accept payment for what I did," the Scottish farmer replied, waving off the offer. At that moment, the farmer's son came to the door of the family hovel.

"Is that your son?" the nobleman asked.

"Yes," the farmer replied proudly.

"I'll make you a deal. Let me provide him with the level of education that my son will enjoy. If the lad is anything like his father, he'll no doubt grow to be a man we both will be proud of." And that he did.

Farmer Fleming's son attended the very best schools and in time, he graduated from St. Mary's Hospital Medical School, London University, and went on to become known throughout the world as the noted Sir Alexander Fleming, the man who discovered penicillin.

Years afterward, the same nobleman's son who was saved from the bog was stricken with pneumonia. What saved his life this time? Penicillin. The name of the nobleman? Lord Randolph Churchill. His son's name? Sir Winston Churchill.

What force is operating here? It's the same one that seeks to work with us when we choose to live the inspired life we signed up for.

6. When You Are Inspired . . .
You Discover Yourself to Be a Greater Person by Far
Than You Ever Dreamed Yourself to Be

The act of being inspired by some great purpose allows us to feel the essence of a spiritual being having a human experience, rather than the other way around. Patanjali suggests that we could never even dream of our greatness because we've been imprisoned by our beliefs about who we are. We've bought into the idea that we were limited in our ability to create an all-encompassing life, and we were certain that we had no choice in our own destiny. We defended our need to acquire more and to live a scarcity consciousness in which we competed with everyone else for a meager slice of the whole pie. All of these imprisoning thoughts result when we're not guided by Spirit.

Moving into a state of inspiration removes all of those restraining ideas. As Patanjali notes, we'll discover someone we couldn't imagine because we were incarcerated in ego's jail, imprisoned by what we now recognize from our inspired viewpoint is an illusion. The poet Rabindranath Tagore (winner of the Nobel Prize for Literature in 1913) writes of those who live exclusively in the false identity of the ego: "He who, in the world of men, goes about singing for alms from door to door, with his one-stringed instrument and long robe of patched-up rags on his back." Tagore is describing how limited our thoughts and our lives are when we're not in-Spirit.

As we move toward heeding the ultimate calling, we no longer live exclusively "in the world of men," so we know that we all have greatness awaiting us. We need to awaken from the bad dream that has stupefied us in the fog of ego, and live from the blissful perspective offered by being in-Spirit.

Some Suggestions for Putting the Ideas in This Chapter to Work for You

— Monitor your thoughts for any that put bonds on your ability to manifest. Even a seemingly insignificant one that questions your resolve to live in-Spirit represents an energy vibration that inhibits you from creating your desires. Change a thought from *This is unlikely to happen because I've never been lucky before* to *What I need is on its way; I'm going to look everywhere for evidence that I'm aligned with the same energy vibrations as my desire.* Be alert for thoughts that creep in by force of habit and reflect the idea that you can't manifest your desires.

— Repeat this mantra to yourself as often as you can, making it a ritual that only you are privy to: *I have absolutely no limits on what I intend to create.* By repeating these words, you'll find that you slip into the world of Spirit where limitlessness defines all reality.

— Make an attempt to spend some time each day in a state of meditation, wherein you let go of all ideas about time, space, and linear directionality. Just allow yourself to be. . . . Imagine yourself without a body or any possessions and attachments—in this way, you'll begin to emulate the world of Spirit. It's out of this nondirectionality, with no backward or forward, up or down, or north and south, that you'll brush right up against inspiration. Such a feeling may come out of nowhere, but it will appear when you do everything you can to emulate connectedness with Spirit.

— Develop a private trust in your ability to activate and attract dormant forces. Visualize yourself as a being who can command these seemingly inert forces to work with you. Remind yourself of this truth: *If I stay in harmony with my originating Spirit, that invisible All-Creating Force will go to work on my behalf.* Just know this within. Then begin to look for even the slightest hint that those hibernating forces are awakening from their apparent slumber to work with you. In reality, these forces never sleep; rather, they only work with you when you're a vibrational match to them. So change your expectations for yourself—expect the best, expect guidance, expect your fortunes to change, expect a miracle!

* * *

Remember the words of Michelangelo: "The greater danger for most of us lies not in setting our aim too high and falling short; but in setting our aim too low, and achieving our mark." When you were in-Spirit prior to materializing, your aim was high and your expectations were God-like. Reacquaint yourself with that vision and begin living an inspired life . . . just turn the page to begin.

CHAPTER 5

FINDING YOUR WAY TO AN INSPIRED LIFE

"If we examine every stage of our lives, we find that from our first breath to our last we are under the constraint of circumstances. And yet we still possess the greatest of all freedoms, the power of developing our innermost selves in harmony with the moral order of the Universe, and so winning peace at heart whatever obstacles we meet.

"It is easy to say this and to write this. But it always remains a task to which every day must be devoted. Every morning cries to us: 'Do what you ought and trust what may be.'"

— JOHANN WOLFGANG VON GOETHE

WHEN I SPEAK ABOUT INSPIRATION AND PURPOSE, I frequently hear people ask, "But what if I don't really know what would inspire me?" or "How do I find my purpose when nothing seems to resonate with me at the level of bliss you speak about?" That's why this chapter and the following one are dedicated to my heartfelt answers to these questions, which seem most bothersome to those who'd really love to heed their ultimate calling.

Just the mere act of questioning our ability to live an inspired life represents resistance that we need to examine because it implies that we're deficient in our spiritual quest. Of course, nothing could be further from the truth: In the world of Spirit from whence we came, there are no deficits, lacks, or shortages; and there's definitely no such thing as purposelessness. This is an intelligent system that we're a part of—we're Divine beings who are a piece of the entire pie of creation. By questioning our ability to activate a connection to inspiration, we give evidence of our lack of belief in our divinity. With this minor reproach in mind, I'll now explain ways to believe in, and connect with, our ultimate calling.

First, in order to put to rest any question regarding our personal right to live an inspired life, we must claim our divinity. The fundamental truth each of us needs to affirm is: *I am a Divine creation. All creation has purpose. I am here to be like God.* We should tattoo this statement on our consciousness and wear it proudly!

We must begin the process of getting in-Spirit with a firm declaration from which we never waver. Here's a poetic reminder of this truth from Walt Whitman: ". . . perhaps the deepest, most eternal thought latent in the human soul [is] the thought of God, merged in the thoughts of moral right and the immortality of identity. Great, great is this thought—aye, greater than all else."

Yes, as Whitman says, this thought of being merged with God is greater than any we could ever have. Once we've accepted this, we can move on to knowing why we're here and what inspires us. We can begin to trust in the intelligence that beats our heart 50 or 60 times every minute and at the same time turns the earth once every 24 hours, keeps the planets aligned, and creates every millisecond. Our job is to be as much like the Source of All Being as we can, and the nagging questions about what inspires us and why we're here dissolve in this grand desire. Once we declare our holy, Divine nature to be our essence, rather than something to be verified, it all seems so obvious: The journey to feeling purposeful and inspired begins by seeking to be like God in all of our thoughts and actions.

I quoted Goethe at the beginning of the chapter because I consider him to be among the most intellectually and spiritually gifted Renaissance men who ever lived. Study his words thoughtfully as you read this chapter, and keep in mind that every one of us is capable of being inspired every day of our life; after all, this is our entitlement offered by God, with Whom we collaborated before ever arriving here.

Sharing Is Inspiration

Oneness with our Source is achieved by becoming like It, and Its essence is giving and sharing. Therefore, in order to know our purpose and heed our ultimate call to inspiration, we must also become a being who's more focused on sharing than on receiving.

This Universe works on the Law of Attraction—so the more we shift the focus from our desires to wanting more for others, the richer we become. When we tell the Universe to "Gimme, gimme, gimme," it responds in like fashion, and we find ourselves feeling put upon and out of balance. But when we ask the Universe, "How may I share?" it will ask, "How may *I* share with *you?* You are a being of sharing, and I return the same energy back to you."

Now this may at first seem absurd, particularly if we've been raised on an ego consciousness that's stressed the need to "look out for number one," and "get what I can before someone else does." But I assure you that when we make the transformation to a being of sharing, the question of how to become inspired will disappear. So whenever we find ourselves "wanting more," the solution is to do more for society, for humanity, or for the environment. Any act of sharing as a response to our wants leads to feeling inspired. The fact is, it just plain feels good to do something for others.

When I completed writing *The Power of Intention* a couple of years ago, for instance, I had such a glorious feeling of having been guided through the writing that I wanted to express my gratitude in some way other than taking credit for it or thinking about myself. That's when I thought of my personal editor, Joanna Pyle, who has taken my disjointed thoughts and ramblings and turned them into cohesive books for almost three decades. I knew that in all of her 65 years, my friend had never known the joy of owning a new car—it simply hadn't been a priority in her life. So I arranged for Joanna to receive a brand-new camper van as an expression of my gratitude for all of her brilliant editing, going back to the 1970s. In that single act of sharing, I received as much joy and fulfillment as I did from writing the contents of a book that consumed me for almost a year.

Understand that this isn't necessarily about giving our possessions or money away; rather, it's about living in the same vibrational energy as our Source and attracting that energy in each other. It's about thinking of others before ourselves and offering the love we feel for all of life, first in our thoughts and then in our actions . . . and that's how we make a connection to inspiration. This is because we've become one with our Source in thought and then action, or as Goethe puts it so perfectly, "[W]e still possess the greatest of all freedoms, the power of developing our innermost selves in harmony with the moral order of the Universe, and so winning peace at heart." A being of sharing frequently thinks in those terms.

When we contemplate our Creator, we realize that God simply gives and imparts without demanding anything in return. We aren't required to give to, pay homage to, or do anything for God. It's *our* demands that distance us from feeling inspired—so we need to let go of them and extend ourselves in an attitude of sharing. I speak here of an inner transformation in which extending love outward is our predominant disposition. This can take the form of a silent blessing toward someone we might have previously judged, a loving greeting, a kind remark, or a thought wishing the highest good for all concerned. As simple as it sounds, this is the ultimate impetus for feeling inspired.

Blocking the Bliss of Inspiration

The most frequent lament I hear from people who want to feel inspired is, "I don't have any idea what I should be doing, so how can I find my inspiration?" My answer is always the same: "Inspiration isn't what we receive from what we do—it's what we bring to our actions." In other words, when we're living in-Spirit, we can feel inspired doing anything. Our job is to stay connected to our spiritual essence, rather than looking for a position that we think will provide us with that connection.

When we feel confused about what we should do to feel inspired, it's time to go to a quiet place. It could be in our home, down by the sea, in a meadow, or deep in the woods—it just needs to be a place where we can be alone with God. Once there, we can imagine talking to our beloved Creator, Who's trusted more than anyone else. Conversing with God will just affirm the answers we already have within us, and we can then awaken to a realization of what we're to do. It isn't about getting the right job—whatever we're doing at the moment provides us with a unique opportunity to bring inspiration to our workplace. We can do this by becoming a being of sharing and extending the love we came from to everyone we encounter, particularly those who seem to be the most annoying or those we tend to blame for our absence of inspiration.

Basically, we have two choices for meeting any problem that seems to be blocking us from the bliss of inspiration. The first choice is *the way of frailty,* in which we assure ourselves that we're weak and incapable. Frustration, grief, fears, and tears are the hallmarks of this choice, wherein we attempt to cure a wrong with another wrong. The frailty method multiplies tensions by focusing on what's missing, and often invites the advice of others in an attempt to resolve our inner tension and lack of inspiration.

The second choice is *to go within* and know that at our core, beyond all physical and mental factors, there resides the Spirit that's always connected to God. Any problem, and I emphasize *any* problem, represents our inability to consciously connect to our Source in the moment. With a conscious connection, we don't seek the advice of others, we seek *information*—so our decisions are made between ourselves and our Creator. We frequently have quiet interchanges with God, and we know and trust that spiritual guidance is available as an alignment of energy.

When we feel uninspired, we recognize that we need to make a vibrational adjustment that puts our thoughts and behaviors back in alignment with the *desire* to be inspired. Then when this realignment takes place, we can laugh at the folly of seeking something outside of ourselves (such as an activity or a job) to inspire us. By simply realigning and harmonizing with Spirit, we let inspiration blossom in the field of harmony.

Listening to the Voice of God

When we make the decision to become a being of sharing, and practice keeping our thoughts harmonized with Spirit energy on a daily basis, our purpose will not only find us, it will *chase after* us wherever we go. Since we've become aligned with our Creator, we won't be able to escape it. You see, when we live as much of life as possible in God-realization, nothing can go wrong. What and who we need will surface, and we'll notice that we can't escape feeling that something much greater than our individual life is at work within and around us.

Our number one relationship must be to this creative energy of God. When we go to our Source, we activate the energy that reconnects us to our purpose—inspiration then shows up right before our eyes, even when we may have stopped thinking about it. Our purpose manifests in many ways and won't be limited to a career slot; in fact, it's often something that requires us to leave a particular kind of employment to pursue something we'd never considered.

We must trust that inspiration is already here—it only eludes us because we've disconnected in some way from the Spirit that was and always will be our essence. I recently received a letter from a woman in Kansas that illustrates this message perfectly. Just out of the blue, she felt compelled to do something that she'd never contemplated before, and *voilà!*—she was inspired and remains so today. With Gail's permission, here is her letter, which has been edited for clarity. (For more on Japa, which is a form of meditation, please see my book *Getting in the Gap*.)

> *Dear Wayne,*
> *Thank you so much for your presentations and tapes. You are frequently my traveling companion as I drive in my job. I just wanted to add my testimony to the power of Japa.*
> *I was an on-and-off meditator but realized how much more smoothly my days went when I was "on" it. I visited Kenya, Africa, in June of 2002 and met an eight-year-old orphan girl there. As I sat on the ground, she crawled into my lap, and a*

voice said, "Take her home." I physically turned around, but
no one was there. Again the voice said, "Take her home." I
asked my 18-year-old daughter (who was with me on the trip)
what she thought about my adopting this beautiful child.
With the quickness of a sprinter, she replied, "Go for it."

When we returned to the States a week later, I realized
that if I didn't follow through with this adoption, I'd always
regret it. Regret seemed much larger than the task of adopting!
I began doing Japa each morning, and through a series of
miracles, that special little girl was able to come to this country.
I named her Nellie, and she has been a blessing to me and my
other children.

Nellie's adoption was part two of God's plan. Part one had
unfolded a couple of years before, when I felt guided to sponsor
a series of workshops for which I profited $10,000 with very
little time or work. And guess what the final cost of adopting
Nellie was? The first time I heard the voice, I chose to disregard
it and/or think it through, making lists of pros and cons. But I
could not rest until I proceeded with the workshops. That's how
I explained to my family that I needed to proceed with adopting
Nellie—obedience had brought abundance into our lives, and
now it was time to share that abundance. Nellie has brought
the abundance of love and forgiveness into our home. She is
truly a treasure.

Thank you for sharing your gift of this wonderful meditation. It changed my life and the life of a little girl.

Sincerely,
Gail Beale
Topeka, Kansas

Gail used her meditation practice to stay connected to her
Creator and to be open to having her purpose in life find her—
and when a small orphaned child in Kenya crawled into her lap,
purpose did indeed find her. Gail calls this "God's plan," but
she's actually a piece of God. She came from God, so she must be
like what she came from. Hence, God's plan is her plan, and vice

versa. In her meditation practice, Gail heard a voice—that voice belonged to her highest self, the part that never left Spirit, is always inspired, and can be heard when allowed to come through. It's a voice that lives in each and every one of us, too.

Ask, and It Will Be Given

It may sound too simplistic, but the ancient biblical advice to "ask, and it will be given" carries a great message for us as we attempt to find our way to an inspired life. I interpret *to ask* as being identical to allowing the guidance of our Source to flow back to us. Recall that allowing is an absence of resistance, which means that we're in the process of reconnecting to the vibrational energy of Spirit, not making a plea to a disconnected being residing outside of us. When we're in harmony with Spirit, we're just like God, so our desires are the same. In this state, we're asking our highest self to get back into balance and allow our desires to be in this spiritual proportion.

The greater our desire, the more horsepower we'll apply to its fulfillment. This is what true asking is: a plea for the assistance to put into practice that which matches up with our desires. The more intense our desires, the greater the measure of love going into our asking and our labor will be—and coming in contact with love is the very essence of Spirit and inspiration. Weak desire will attract doubt and weakness, which will cause us to experience monotony and drudgery in our efforts. With monotony, we'll give up, but with love, we'll be available to abundant hope.

For example, I find it impossible to think in boring terms when it comes to my writing. My desire is so intense that I feel love for what I'm doing and joyful when I even pass by my writing space. I get a warm feeling throughout my body because my desire to convey these ideas and express what I'm learning each day is so intense that it matches up with the spiritual energy of the Source of All Creation. When I ask, it's for the intensity of my desire to be matched up with my spiritual Source so that I can accomplish that desire. Obviously when I'm asking for guidance, my thoughts or queries go out to my spirit, which then matches up with the Divine Source.

The quality that stands out among those who feel inspired is one of an intense, burning desire—it goes beyond talent and ability as a measure of success. We need to ask this highest part of ourselves to align with Source, and for the intensity of our desire to be so great that our love for who we are and what we do precludes the possibility of any boredom, tedium, or weariness. In this manner, our inspired vision will be forthcoming.

Creating and Holding on to Our Vision

The desire to find our way to inspiration involves creating a vision of living in-Spirit 100 percent of the time. Even if we don't have a clue what we should be doing or what our mission is, we need to practice creating this vision anyway. Our inner picture has to be based on our intention to feel good, which is of course synonymous with feeling *God.*

If we make this an inner mantra: *I intend to feel good,* we can picture ourselves experiencing joy regardless of what's going on around us. We can remind ourselves that whatever we desire is on its way, in amounts greater than ever imagined. If we keep this vision uppermost in mind, then before long, the All-Creating Source will conspire to bring our vision into our physical life. Most important, we'll begin to act on our vision and receive Divine guidance.

Here's a Lao Russell quote that I hold close to my heart:

> Whatever work you perform with deep desire, God will work with you by doing exactly as much for you as you do to manifest Him. The farmers, or gardeners, or foresters know this. They

know that a little work given by them brings but little work done by Nature. The giving and regiving are always equal. The more service you give to Nature, the more Nature will work with you in her regivings.

It all begins and ends with our willingness to hold a desire in our inner vision despite what we see around us now. The inner picture is what we'll ultimately have to act upon, so we want to be very careful about what we create and hold for ourselves. If we see ourselves as limited, unworthy, weak, timid, or sickly, then we'll act on these inner portraits. For example, I was touched by Ram Dass's description of wondering what it would feel like to be old and infirm in his book *Still Here*. He held that thought and almost immediately experienced a stroke, requiring his need for continuous care by others. "Thinking old" attracted the element of old that he so feared.

The truth is that we react to the vision we create and hold— and so do all of the cells in our body. So it's vitally important to hold a clear vision of ourselves as deserving of feeling inspired, knowing that it's our ultimate calling, and choosing to be in-Spirit even when everything around us suggests otherwise. We need to opt to be a being of sharing, living as close to God-realization as is possible. The ancient Persian poet Rumi states this so perfectly with the following lines:

The garden of the world has no limits
except in your mind.

Its presence is more beautiful than the stars,
with more clarity
than the polished mirror of your heart.

Clear your mind of limits, and move into Spirit, Whose presence, as Rumi tells us, is "more beautiful than the stars."

Some Suggestions for Putting
the Ideas in This Chapter
to Work for You

— Practice sharing anonymously. The goal is to be at one with the Creator, and It isn't looking for credit, a reward, or even a thank-you. The more you practice being a sharing person rather than one who continually wonders, *What's in it for me?* the more flows back to you when you least expect it. You don't have to make deals with God in which you perform acts of sharing in exchange for special favors—just work at becoming a being of sharing *with no expectation of receiving anything in return.* You'll be pleasantly surprised at how inspired you'll feel.

— Give yourself the time and quiet space to enter into dialogue with your Source. Be willing to ask the questions that you need to feel guided by Spirit—the answers you seek will come rushing toward you when you're in authentic communication. I've found that very early in the morning is such a powerful time for me that I call it my "being-with-God time." Every morning when I awake, I lie in bed and say, "I'm going to spend a few quiet moments with God and ask for guidance for this day," and I always hear instructions to begin by sharing something with someone. I treasure those 10 or 15 minutes of being with my Source as I start the day in gratitude for being alive, healthy, and able to help others.

— Keep an open mind about what it takes to feel inspired. It may not necessarily mean a change of career; it might simply involve writing your equivalent of *Mr. Holland's Opus*, helping orphaned children, purchasing a horse for riding and competing, or buying a piece of vacant property and planning a vacation getaway spot. However, it is entirely possible that a change in job and location *is* beckoning you, so stay open and allow it to find you. Regardless, you should always stay connected to Spirit and trust the messages you receive.

— Remember this simple truth: *The answer to how is yes.* You may never know exactly how you're going to accomplish the feeling of inspiration, but by saying *yes!* to life and all that calls you, the how will take care of itself.

— Remove inner references and visions of what you don't want. Instead of thinking, *I will not attract sickness into my world,* affirm, *I attract health into my world* and *I will never allow my brain to atrophy; I will stay active throughout all of my life.* Know that you are connected to a continual stream of well-being, and let this knowing guide you in all of your visions for inspiration.

* * *

Here's a question that Ralph Waldo Emerson posed, which I'd like you to ponder before turning to the next section: "We are very near to greatness: one step and we are safe; can we not take the leap?"

One step. Surely you can take one step for your own inspired greatness. . . .

PART II

THE FUNDAMENTALS OF INSPIRATION

"The philosophy of six thousand years has not searched the chambers and magazines of the soul.

"In its experiments there has always remained, in the last analysis, a residuum it could not resolve. Man is a stream whose source is hidden. Our being is descending into us from we know not whence. . . .

"I am constrained every moment to acknowledge a higher origin for events than the will I call mine."

— RALPH WALDO EMERSON
from *"Essay IX: The Over-Soul"*

CHAPTER 6

ESSENTIAL PRINCIPLES FOR FINDING YOUR WAY TO AN INSPIRED LIFE

*"Well, every man has a religion;
has something in heaven or earth which he will give up
everything else for—something which absorbs him—which may
be regarded by others as being useless—yet it is his dream,
it is his lodestar, it is his master. That, whatever it is,
seized upon me, made me its servant, slave—induced me to set
aside the other ambitions—a trail of glory in the heavens,
which I followed, followed with a full heart. . . .
When once I am convinced, I never let go . . ."*

— WALT WHITMAN

THIS CHAPTER PRESENTS SIX PRINCIPLES that are important to observe as we seek an inspired life—they're a blueprint to refer to as we reconstruct a life in-Spirit. I'm listing them in no particular order of importance because I believe that they're equally essential.

Principle #1: Be Independent of the Good Opinion of Others

In order to live in-Spirit, we must adopt Arthur Miller's trust that the Source is always working within us, or Walt Whitman's belief that our ultimate calling "may be regarded by others as being useless—yet it is [our] dream, it is [our] lodestar." In other words, inspiration must be our master, even though following it might disappoint others.

When inspiration makes its presence known, we must pay attention if our priority is to be who or what we were meant to be. William Shakespeare's famous query, "To be or not to be: that is the question," symbolizes the urgent choices that we have to make—that is, do we become what we came here to be, or do we ignore that calling? In this oft-quoted soliloquy, Hamlet delves deeper by wondering, "Whether 'tis nobler in the mind to suffer / The slings and arrows of outrageous fortune, / Or to take arms against a sea of troubles, / And by opposing end them? . . ." Suffering the consequences of living according to someone else's wishes doesn't make any sense; rather, we need to oppose the external opinions that try to force us to be what we're not intended to be.

There are many well-meaning people in our lives who have ideas about what we should or shouldn't be doing . . . relatives tend to be specialists in this area! If we let them guide us with advice that isn't congruent with our inner calling, we'll suffer the anguish—the "slings and arrows"—of an uninspired life. Each of us can feel what we're being called to be; when we listen, we can hear our own impatient voices coaxing us to listen and complete the assignments we brought with us from the world of Spirit. But when we allow the opinions and dictates of others to determine what we're going to be, we lose sight of our objective to live an inspired life.

We need to determine for ourselves how much we've allowed others to decide issues such as what we do, where we live, with whom we live, and even how we're treated. We must know that absolutely no one else truly knows and feels what we're here to accomplish, so we must give ourselves permission to hear our inner guidance and ignore the pressure from others. Regardless of how absurd our inner calling might seem, it's authentically *ours* and doesn't have to make sense to anyone else. The willingness to listen and act on our inspiration, independent of the opinions of others, is imperative.

Principle #2: *Be Willing to Accept the Disapproval of Others*

Logically following the last principle, this one notes that we're going to incur the disfavor of many people when we follow our inclinations to be in-Spirit and live the life we came here to live. This isn't a selfish or cynical attitude: When we begin to follow our ultimate calling, there *will* be a lot of resistance. In fact, the purpose of the "slings and arrows" sent our way is to get us to change our mind and be "reasonable," which translates to "Do it *my* way!"

However, as we gain the strength to ignore the pressure to conform, resistance will diminish and ultimately change to respect. When we steadfastly refuse to think, act, and conform to the mandates of others, the pressure to do so loses its momentum. All we have to do is endure some initial disapproval such as dogmatic persuasion, anger, pouting, silence, and long-winded lectures . . . and then we're on our way to inspiration rather than frustration.

Here's a recent example of this from my own life. I elected to have most of the royalties and all of the advance payments for this book go to a scholarship fund, and there were people who tried to get me to "come to my senses" and not "throw my money away," which was how they viewed my decision. I have an inner voice that is overwhelmingly powerful, and I trust in what truly inspires me. I'd known for many years that one day I'd endow a scholarship fund at my alma mater, for instance—the thought of young, financially challenged students having the opportunity that I'd received as a young military veteran inspires me more than I can relate to you here in these pages. So I was comfortable with, and able to ignore, the disapproval I encountered, giving responses such as, "I know what I'm doing and why I'm doing it," and "Don't waste your time and mine attempting to convince me otherwise." And sure enough, the resistance I met was converted to acceptance.

The people who receive the most approval in life are the ones who care the least about it—so technically, if we want the approval of others, we need to stop caring about it and turn our attention to becoming an inspired being of sharing. One little note of caution here: When we raise our children according to these principles, and they observe us living them on a daily basis, we'll have to deal with their determination to respect their inner calling. For example, when my daughter Sommer was about 11 years old and I asked to see her report card, I was a bit taken aback by her response. "Why do you want to see it?" she asked.

When I said, "Well, I'm your father, and I think I should know how you're doing in school," she matter-of-factly replied, "But these are my grades, not yours, and if I thought you needed to see them, I would've shown them to you already."

I assure you that she wasn't being disrespectful; she simply had no need to share her grades with me. Since I knew that she was doing very well in school, I let it go—and let her be who she wanted to be.

Principle #3: *Stay Detached from Outcomes*

Inspiration doesn't come from completing tasks or meeting goals; in fact, that's the sure way to have it elude us. Returning to Spirit, you see, is an experience of living fully in the present moment. Our purpose in life isn't to arrive at a destination where we find inspiration, just as the purpose of dancing isn't to end up at a particular spot on the floor. The purpose of dancing—and of life—is to enjoy every moment and every step, regardless of where we are when the music ends.

Many of us are seduced into believing that having goals is necessary for a successful life, especially since we've been brainwashed by slogans such as "If you don't know where you're going, how will you know when you're there?" and "Not having a goal is more to be feared than not reaching a goal." This kind of logic keeps us from feeling inspired because we live a life of *striving* while foregoing *arriving*.

A more rewarding spiritual truth is that there's only now—and when this moment passes, it will be replaced by another one, ad infinitum. To use up our "present now" being consumed with a "future now" that will only turn into a "then" is the prescription for the absence of inspiration. Since there's only now, learning to live in it and enjoy every present moment is the same as being in-Spirit, while being focused on an outcome to determine our level of happiness and success keeps us out of Spirit.

Yoga master Sri Swami Sivananda offered the only worthwhile goal I know of when he said that the goal of life is God-realization. Now *here's* a goal I can live with! After all, this allows me to live in-Spirit every moment of my life, while simultaneously thinking ahead to the next God-realized moment (and the next). As the great Indian sage Ramana Maharshi once remarked, "There is no goal to be reached. There is nothing to be attained. You are the Self. You exist always." Now this is real inspiration.

As I sit here writing, I don't have a goal in mind, yet I trust that the book will be completed. I've seen it, even though I'm months away from the final product. I live in the bliss of creating right here, right now, and I relish these moments. I trust that the outcome will be handled by the same Source that inspires these words to appear seemingly out of nowhere. I'm here now—in peace, in love, and in awe—and my only goal is to stay in this consciousness and enjoy every moment, putting into practice what I agreed to when I was in-Spirit before becoming the particle that began this glorious journey.

Principle #4: *Know That We Need Nothing/No Things to Be Inspired*

We came into this world of boundaries from a formless energy field of Spirit. We arrived here with nothing/no things, we'll make our exit with nothing/no things, and our purpose (God-realization) requires nothing/no things. We are all that we need to be inspired and living on purpose, and the things that continue to flow into our life are just symbols of the unlimited abundance of our Source. In other words, these things have no value in and of themselves because everything in the physical world is changing and will dissolve back to nothingness anyway.

The objective Universe is *not* made up of things—it's made up of waves of motion that *simulate* the things we're taught to believe are real. Once we accept that, from an infinite perspective, everything we see in nature isn't really what it seems to be, we're able to convert what we view with our eyes into a knowing about all things. Then we can recognize that the objects we believed we needed to feel inspired are nothing from Spirit's perspective. This is what distinguishes the physical person from the spiritual person, the inspired person from the uninspired person.

We're beings of Spirit, living from mind (rather than the body with all of its inherent restrictions), so if we communicate with God in the language of light and energy, we'll see His tolerant amusement at our preoccupation with the illusion of possessions. We don't need more of anything to become inspired; rather, we need to take our attention away from what we see and move into the miraculous world of Spirit, where joy and bliss await us.

Remember: *We're already connected to everything that we think is missing from our life.* Below and above the ranges that our eyes and ears perceive, the entire activity of creation remains invisible and inaccessible—but when we shift from sensory searching to trusting what we know, we discover the folly of chasing after anything in order to feel inspired. All we need is a conscious re-alignment so that our thoughts begin to match up vibrationally with Spirit, which we know is a part of us already. And our state of inspiration is what allows for this realignment.

When we tune in to what we know rather than what we see, we immediately find that every thought of God is repeated throughout the Universe. We can watch as some things enter our life and others leave, all the while remaining in-Spirit, knowing that all of those things have nothing to do with our state of inspiration. We need nothing more to be inspired, since we're connected to Spirit already. The ancient Persian poet Omar Khayyam offered us these words, which summarize this principle that we don't need another thing to be inspired—it's all right here, right now:

> *Forget the day that has been cut off*
> *from thy existence;*
> *disturb not thyself about tomorrow,*
> *which has not yet come,*
> *rest not upon that which is no more;*
> *live happily one instant,*
> *and throw not thy life to the winds.*

Principle #5: *"Don't Die Wondering"*

This principle is extremely important in working toward an inspired life because it motivates us to act—after all, we don't want to be full of regrets because we failed to heed our ultimate calling. Attempting to do something, even if it doesn't succeed, is inspiring because we don't tend to regret what we do, we regret what we *didn't* do. Even following a futile attempt, we're inspired because we know that we gave it a shot. It's wondering whether we should or shouldn't try something that leaves us feeling stressed and incomplete.

When I'm playing a tennis match and being tentative in anticipation of losing a point, for example, I've created a situation in which I'll wonder what kind of a game it would have been had I really gone for it. It's in these moments that I remind myself, "Don't die wondering."

Inspiration has nothing to do with whether we win or lose; in fact, if we just play the game of life, we'll have plenty of wins and losses, regardless of our talent level. If we fail to even try because of fear of rejection or doubt about our talent, we're going to go through life wondering, and that's what keeps us from finding and feeling inspiration.

Most of us, myself included, can remember the intensity of our first romantic attraction—just as we can recall what happened when we didn't follow our inspiration. I've always wondered what would have happened if I'd been able to act on that strong inner call in high school, when I had an enormous crush on a beautiful girl named Janice Nelson. I wanted to ask her out, but I let my fear of being rejected keep me from taking the steps to act upon my inner desires.

On several occasions I even dialed her phone number and hung up when she answered. I never overcame my foreboding thoughts and, in effect, was left to die wondering.

Many years later, I danced with Janice at our 30-year high school reunion and told her how I felt back then. I even confessed the way I'd hang up the phone because of my trepidation. Janice, to my everlasting delight—and chagrin—said, "*I* always had a crush on *you*. I would've loved to have gone out with you, and in fact I tried to leave you clues to call me. But you never did." *Ouch!* That's a perfect example of regretting what I didn't do.

Goethe, writing in *Faust*, provides a poetic description of the two souls living within us: one, a spirit that allows us to make the phone call and ask for the date regardless of the outcome, and the other that clings to the world of fear, and lives to die wondering:

> *Alas, two souls are living in my breast,*
> *And one wants to separate itself from the other.*
> *One holds fast to the world with earthy passion*
> *And clings with twining tendrils:*
> *The other lifts itself with forceful craving*
> *To the very roof of heaven.*

If we lift ourselves "with forceful craving to the very roof of heaven," we'll never die wondering.

Principle #6: *Remember That Our Desires*
Won't Arrive by Our Schedule

There's an ancient aphorism that goes: "If you really want to make God laugh, tell Him your plans." In essence this means that all we desire will arrive in our life when and only when we're aligned vibrationally with the energy of our Source. Our ego won't be consulted or get to determine the schedule—the Creator reveals Its secrets when It's good and ready. Our job is to take the focus off of the *when* and put it on being connected to our originating

Spirit. Our job is to stop challenging and demanding responses from God, and instead be more like Him. Our job is to understand and accept that all of the things that show up in our life, which we often find contradictory or troublesome, are there because we've attracted them . . . and we need to have these obstacles in order to clear an opening for our true Spirit purpose to emerge. This may require a change in thinking patterns, which is something Tom Barber knows all too well.

Tom is the head golf pro at Griffith Park in Los Angeles and owns and operates the Tom Barber Golf Center in Southern California; his father, Jerry, was the PGA champion in 1961. Tom is a close friend whom I can talk to straight about virtually anything. For example, he once admitted to me that business had fallen off, and he was concerned about a deterioration in income due to fewer customers golfing in an economy on the downturn.

He'd gone on for about as long as I was willing to absorb this kind of energy when I finally said, "Tom, you're approaching the whole issue from a perspective that almost guarantees that this financial headache will continue to grow. Try affirming: *What I desire is on its way. It will arrive precisely on God's timetable, not on mine. Everything that I'm experiencing now is disguised as a problem, but I know that it's a blessing. What I desire is on its way, and it's coming to me in amounts even greater that I can imagine. This is my vision, and I'll hold on to it in a state of gratitude, no matter what.*"

I received a letter from my friend about two months after our conversation, in which he wrote: "Thanks for the pep talk. Once I started to say that the business I'm seeking and the finances I need are on their way, everything started to turn around." What happened is that Tom decided to align with the unrestricted abundance of Spirit energy.

As you can see from Tom's example, rather than making demands of God to follow our schedule in order to feel inspired, we can let go, surrender, and remind ourselves that all is in Divine order. We're much more successful when we allow inspiration to flow in on God's terms than when we're impatient and demanding. As always, our job in God-realization is to become more like God—that means surrendering to the timetable that's always perfect, even when it seems to be full of errors.

Keep these six principles handy and access them anytime you find yourself lacking inspiration. Remember, too, that we're called to this world of inspiration, which beckons us to "let go and let God," as they say in the recovery movement. I also love this advice, which was tendered by one of my favorite teachers, Napoleon Hill: "If you can't do great things, do small things in a great way. Don't wait for great opportunities. Seize common, everyday ones and make them great."

Some Suggestions for Putting the Ideas in This Chapter to Work for You

— Make a written commitment to be free of the pressures of people who try to dictate the course of your life, such as: *I intend to listen to my own thoughts concerning my life. I'll be receptive to advice, but I'll do what my conscience dictates, even if I incur disapproval.* By writing your intentions and having them readily available to refer to, you nurture the inspirational energy to follow through on your interests. The intention behind the words guides and reminds you to be steadfast about seeking your own inspiration. Don't employ anger or aggression as ways of being independent of others' opinions—you're Spirit energy from a field of love, and you must *be* love in order to be in-Spirit.

— Small steps will activate matching vibrations to what you desire. So if you want to live close to nature, plan a visit to the place of your dreams and take the small steps to experience what it feels like. If you can't or won't do that, or if you aren't ready to go yet, you can read books or rent movies in order to have the experience vicariously. But be alert to the vibrational energy of thought and action that you offer Spirit.

When my daughter Skye wanted to produce a CD of her own compositions, it seemed like a daunting task to write, perform, record, and arrange for all of the studio time and musicians. She continued to shy away from what inspired her, so I encouraged her to take a small step and write just one song. I gave her a suggestion for a title and gave her a deadline—and then I watched with joy and pride as she sat at her piano, engrossed in her inspiration, creating. One small step put her on the path of inspiration, as Napoleon Hill suggested.

— Instead of goals, make the commitment to live joyfully in the moment. Stop dreaming about the future and get back to the only thing any of us have: now. Decide to live fully in the present, withdrawing attention from past and future. Your desire for inspiration activates the world of Spirit from which you came. Your imagined future, the stuff of goals, is an unnecessary way of squandering the present moment. *Be Here Now* is more than a great book title by Ram Dass, it's the essence of inspiration. Being in the now is the way to remove anxiety, stress, and even some illnesses.

As I sit here writing, I can daydream all I want about completing this book, but in reality, all I can really do (which is precisely what I *am* doing) is listen to my inner voice, offer a matching vibration to those inner pleadings, and feel the joy of allowing the thoughts to come through me onto the pages. The "goal" has been suspended in favor of being here now, living out what I'm being directed by my "Senior Partner" to do. The end result takes care of itself, particularly since I see the end result in my mind, and I use my present moments in harmony with that vision.

— Respect the silent and burning desire that's within you—don't scoff at it, and refuse to be critical or judgmental. Create a sacred space within your home, some private corner where you can have an altar for the symbolic residence of your inner vision. When you walk by this altar, offer a silent blessing and express gratitude for the presence of inspiration in your life. The altar can have photographs, magazine articles, artifacts, totems, crystals, jewelry, plaques . . . anything that reminds you of your own passions. As "silly" or "far-fetched" as this might appear, it's nevertheless true that when you talk and live with daily reminders of Spirit, you become a vibrational match to your ultimate calling.

When I was much younger, many people ridiculed and disregarded my vision of being a writer and a performer, but I treated my inner vision with the veneration that the sacred deserves. Holding my inner knowing in high esteem during my teen years allowed me to undertake writing a novel, irrespective of what anyone around me expressed. When you trust in *your* inner vision, you're trusting the same wisdom that created you.

— Make an affirmation that whatever brings passion, enthusiasm, and inspiration to you is on its way. Say it often: *It is on its way, it will arrive on time, and it will arrive in greater amounts than I imagined.* Then look for even the tiniest clue that will help you be a vibrational match with your affirmation. You'll get what you think about, whether you want it or not!

* * *

The words of a man who was both a philosopher and a Roman emperor will close this chapter. Marcus Aurelius disdained thoughts of violence and refused to go to war; in fact, he presided over his empire with a philosophy of peace and respect for all of his fellow men. Here, he speaks of the things we've forgotten when we're uninspired or not focused in-Spirit.

> When thou art troubled about anything, thou hast forgotten this, that all things happen according to the universal nature; and forgotten this, that a man's wrongful act is nothing to thee; and further thou hast forgotten this, that everything which happens, always happened so and will happen so, and now happens so everywhere; forgotten this too, how close is the kinship between

a man and the whole human race, for it is a community, not of a little blood or seed, but of intelligence. And thou hast forgotten this too, that every man's intelligence is a god, and is an efflux of the deity; and forgotten this, that nothing is a man's own, but that his child and his body and his very soul came from the deity; forgotten this, that everything is opinion; and lastly thou hast forgotten that every man lives the present time only, and loses only this.

Use his words as an inventory of things to remember as you seek to find your way back to inspiration.

CHAPTER 7

INSPIRATION AND YOUR OWN MAGNIFICENCE

*"What is necessary to change a person
is to change his awareness of himself."*

— ABRAHAM MASLOW

*"You are a primary existence. You are a distinct portion
of the essence of God, and contain a certain part of Him
in yourself. Why then are you ignorant of your noble birth?
You carry a God about within you, poor wretch,
and know nothing of it."*

— EPICTETUS

IN THIS CHAPTER, we'll look at our Divine magnificence and examine the ways in which we can view ourselves in these terms for the rest of our life.

It's imperative to eliminate self-perceptions that might cloud our vision or make us question our Divine magnificence. The quote from Abraham Maslow above sets the tone for what we can do: If we want to move from disenchantment to inspiration, or from apathy and indifference to passion and enthusiasm, then it's necessary to alter our awareness of ourselves.

I'm a people watcher, and every day of my life I observe how others carry themselves and treat their body, what they eat, and how they move; I also listen carefully to the seemingly nonchalant verbal utterances that reflect their opinion of themselves. I'm fascinated by what people think of themselves—it's the rare individual who reflects the image that Epictetus describes in the opening quotation.

So what prevents us from seeing ourselves as containing "the essence of God" and knowing that we're of "noble birth"? Only ego, and only when we allow it. A non-ego-based point of view must be firmly in place on the journey to an inspired, passionate life. We must make a decision to see ourselves in the same manner that we knew to be true when we were in the formless dimension contemplating our transformation into a physical being with a purpose.

Who am I? is *the* "big question." We're so accustomed to identifying ourselves by what we have, what we accomplish, what we earn, and what others think of us that we've lost touch with our original self. The answer to this question is: *I'm a unique portion of the essence of God. I originated in-Spirit, yet I've forgotten this fundamental truth.* With this kind of awareness, we'd all be determined to seek our ultimate calling and live an inspired life. Our perception of ourselves would be of a spiritual being who's free of limitations and who trusts that Divine guidance is available at every moment. If we don't currently feel this way, then it's vital that we do what Dr. Maslow suggests and change it.

Changing Our Awareness of Ourselves

How would we think and act in daily life if we were truly aware of our Divine essence? Obviously there wouldn't be room to reproach ourselves because we wouldn't doubt our abilities. In fact, we'd never look in the mirror and feel anything but love and appreciation: We'd see ourselves as fully capable of attracting all we desire; we'd treat our body with reverence and care, giving thanks for its Divine design; we'd celebrate every thought we have, knowing its Divine origin; and we'd become aware of our enormous talents and be awed by all that we are.

We need to encourage the awareness of our magnificence in every regard. When that awareness has been reawakened, the seedlings of inspiration will begin blossoming. Here's a way of expressing these fundamental truths, offered to us by the writings of Bahaullah, of the Baha'i faith: "This most great, this fathomless and surging Ocean is near, astonishingly near, unto you. Behold it is closer to you than your life-vein! Swift as the twinkling of an eye ye can, if ye but wish it, reach and partake of this imperishable favor, this God-given grace, this incorruptible gift, this most potent and unspeakably glorious bounty."

There's no way to be in-Spirit without a changed awareness—so when we accomplish this, we give ourselves the gift of moving from being flawed, limited, lacking, and imperfect to being completely comfortable with our magnificence.

This unspeakably glorious bounty is so close to us . . . all we have to do is to make a few "twinkling-of-an-eye" adjustments, so why not begin now?

Following are three of the most obvious and important changes in awareness that we can make.

1. Changing the Awareness of Our Magnificent Talents and Abilities

I want to emphasize an extremely important point: I'm not writing about self-esteem here, nor am I referring to levels of confidence. Rather, I'm saying that we need to keep the important question *Who am I?* in the forefront of our mind. This question doesn't revolve around previous life experiences, has nothing to do with what we've been told our special qualities or unique abilities are, and isn't related to how worthy or worthless we feel about ourselves—it has to do with a simple truth.

As Epictetus, a philosopher in the 1st century A.D. said, "You carry a God about within you, poor wretch, and know nothing of it." Just like Epictetus, who was born into slavery yet became one of our most profound teachers, we came into this world with an inexhaustible supply of talent. Our abilities are as limitless as God's are because we're a distinct portion of the essence of Him—and there's an infallible way to begin entertaining those abilities and creating as He does.

That way is to become aware that anything that excites us is a clue that we have the ability to pursue it. Anything that truly intrigues us is evidence of a Divine (albeit latent) talent that's signaling our awareness. Having an interest in something is the clue to a thought that's connected to our calling—that thought is a vibration of energy in this vast Universe. If something *really* appeals to us and we feel excited, but perceive ourselves as devoid of the talent we think is necessary, it's probably an even higher vibration.

Anything that's causing excitement within us is evidence of a Spirit message that's saying, "You can do this—yes, you can!" If we react to this message with anything other than "You're correct—I *can* do this! I have the ability to do it," then we've selected the vibration of resistance and ignored the vibration of excitement and interest that spoke to us.

How could it be any other way? We wouldn't think of things that are interesting and exciting to us if we didn't have the inherent ability to act on these thoughts, especially since we're a portion of the All-Creating, All-Capable, All-Wise Force. Just the fact that we're interested and excited about doing something is all the evidence we need—this is inspiration right in front of us, begging us to pay attention to the feeling. Therefore, we need to change our awareness in order to take note of our stimulation, rather than of the opinions of others. We need to ignore the scores on some standardized test, or worse yet, our own inventory of past experiences that led us to conclude that we're untalented and incapable.

Our thoughts about who we are, what excites us, and what we feel called to be and do are all Divinely inspired and come with whatever guidance and assistance we'll need to actualize these goals. The decision at this point is: Are we willing to listen to these Divine thoughts that pique our interest, or do we go on listening to the false self that's made us what Epictetus called a "poor wretch"?

* * *

Rather than case studies of which I have only secondhand knowledge, I'm going to use some examples from my own life that illustrate listening to the false self.

My background would appear to be an unlikely one for what I'm calling *magnificence*. Here's what it would look like on paper: *Fathered by an alcoholic who abandoned his three children; childhood years spent in foster homes; a classic underachiever educated in public schools; grew up at the low end of the socioeconomic scale; no financial advantages; no examples of, or ambitions for, higher education; four years as an enlisted man in the United States Navy; admitted to a university on a provisional acceptance at the age of 22 due to lower-than-average grades in high school; worked his way through three advanced degrees by being a cashier and stock boy in a grocery store in Detroit.* This isn't exactly what you'd call a prescription for becoming the best-selling author of 25 books and a successful public speaker.

I couldn't begin to tell you how many teachers of creative writing and speech gave me low grades for my efforts in these fields. All I can say for certain is that I've always had a knowing about my interest in writing, and have been excited by the prospect of entertaining and informing an audience—any audience! By all of the "accepted" standards, I didn't have any writing ability. What I did have (and still do) was an interest and a passion for writing: It inspired and thrilled me, and I simply loved it. From the perspective of inspiration, I had the ability to do it, and that's all I needed to know.

Then, as now, I trusted that the Universe would handle all of the details, including: *Will I be published? Will the critics approve? Will my book be a bestseller? Will my mother approve? Will I get an apology from any of my old English teachers?* But really, who cares about all this? The fact that writing excites me is all I've ever needed to know. When I follow that thought and stay with it, I conclude that I have the ability and the talent . . . and so do you.

Like me, it's easy to find what excites you. What do you find intriguing? Does learning yoga and becoming an instructor interest you? Then you have your answer. The issue isn't about ability, it's about being matched up in-Spirit with your current thoughts and behaviors. I still remember the excitement I felt at being admitted to a doctoral program. Despite the fact that no one in my family had ever entertained such a possibility and I didn't know one single person who had entered, let alone completed, an advanced-degree program, I was excited beyond what I can convey to you here. I knew that whatever I needed in the way of ability and talent would be there.

So how about you—do you live with resistance, or do you allow your enthusiasm and excitement to be a vibrational match to what intrigues you? Keep in mind that as one of God's glorious thoughts, you've originated out of an energy field that knows only possibility. So stay in vibrational harmony with this idea and know that your thoughts—which emerge as interests, excitement, inner thrills, and illuminating sensations—are indications that you have the necessary ability to merge with your magnificent creativity. You came from magnificence, and you are magnificent still.

2. Changing the Awareness of
Our Magnificent Physical Presence

During the writing of this book, I was engaged in a passionate tennis match when I overheard a woman on her cell phone saying, "I can't believe she would even say something like that—she's such an unattractive person herself." I was getting ready to serve the ball to my opponent and actually had to stop to make a note to write about this incident and the question it raises. *How is it possible for a creation of God to be unattractive in any way?* I wondered.

I thought about an apple pie: One slice must be the same as the entire pie—it can't suddenly be pineapple or banana. The same logic applies to all of us: If we came from Source, how is it possible for us to be different from It? I doubt that the woman on the cell phone would ever deign to call God unattractive, yet that's exactly what she was inadvertently doing. And we do the very same thing when we place pejorative labels on our body, the magnificent temple we occupy.

In the previous section, we answered the question *Who am I?* in spiritual rather than physical terms. Now let's ask a similar question regarding our physical body. Even though we've been living in it ever since we began as an embryo, it's still relevant to ask, *What is this body that emerged from Spirit?*

Our body is made up of chemicals, far too many for me to elaborate here, but some of them are iron, magnesium, calcium, nitrogen, hydrogen . . . and on and on goes the list. These chemicals are part of a finite supply here on Earth, so what flows through our veins is part of that finite supply. To that end, the iron that's in our blood was once somewhere else—perhaps in a dinosaur, in the body of Jesus, or in a mountain in Afghanistan—and now it's in our body. And when we leave our body, our iron supply will reside someplace else on Earth as a part of that finite supply.

In other words, our entire planet is made up of the exact same chemicals that constitute our physical makeup. Chemically speaking, there's no difference between humans and rocks, trees, orangutans, or distant stars—grind them all up and their chemical composition isn't what distinguishes one from the other. Our physical presence is a spiritually directed conglomeration of a hodgepodge of chemicals, and the end result is that we're beings made up of the same stuff that makes up the stars. We're made up of stardust. That's right, the stuff of dreams—twinkling, magical, beautiful, light-filled stardust!

Remember that the Spirit from which we originated can create anything, including worlds, so why would it choose ugly or unattractive creations? We're here in the perfect body for our time in this incarnation, and it's a living, breathing miracle in every way. It's guided and being directed by an invisible Force that directs everything and everyone in the Universe: It beats our heart, digests our food, circulates our blood, grows our hair, and repairs our cuts and bruises, all independent of our opinions.

I wrote earlier about being independent of the opinions of others. Well, we aren't beautiful or attractive because of how we stack up against a runway model—we're beautiful because we came from beauty, so we must be the same as what we came from. All labels such as *unattractive, ugly, homely,* and *unbecoming* (as well as *pretty, attractive, handsome,* and *beautiful*) are judgments designed to compare one person to another using artificial standards set up by ego-dominated people and organizations.

Living in-Spirit means that we see our body with all of its unique characteristics and feel thankful for the perfect temple that's temporarily housing our true "primary existence." If it's short or tall, bald or hairy, stumpy or slender, extend loving appreciation to it every day. If it can't see or hear, resides in a wheelchair or a hospital bed, has crooked teeth or only three toes—whatever—love this collection of stardust! A prayerful thought might go like this: *I think of my body as a piece of the eternal, an individualized expression of God. I live in-Spirit, inspired because I'm the same as the loving energy that created me, which is perfect.*

Think about the logic of what I'm saying here. Obviously we can't live a life of inspiration if the physical shell we take with us everywhere is perceived as anything other than a Divine, perfect creation. Our attitude toward our body, along with how we feed and exercise it, must match up with Spirit. We came from love, so we must extend that love and appreciation to our body at all times in order to be genuinely inspired.

3. Changing the Awareness of Our Magnificent Personal History

This third and final element of our inspirational magnificence is perhaps our greatest challenge. How can we look upon all that we've done (or failed to do) and view it through the lens of our magnificence, especially when we've been trained to feel shame and self-reproach as a result of our perceived failures or flaws. Early on we're taught to evaluate our worth as a human being based on how well we fit in, what grades we get, and what merit badges we acquire. Then, as adults, we're measured by the amount of money we make, the promotions we receive, whom we've pleased or disappointed, and what sins we've committed. On and on goes this ego-dominated list of judgments that we've had imposed on us and have imposed on ourselves.

At this stage, we need to view our past from the perspective of everything that we've ever done or not done being over. We can't *un*do or *re*do it—we have the choice to look back at the past either through eyes clouded by ego judgments or through an inspired point of view. We can forgive ourselves or we can shame ourselves. Since our goal is to be more like our Creative Source, which is loving and giving, we should adopt forgiveness—but this isn't in ego's script.

We've all reacted to situations in the past in ways that we wouldn't want to today. I personally have done many things that I wouldn't choose to repeat—yet every recovering or recovered addict looks back with gratitude for the experience that brought him or her to a higher, more loving, sober place. As I've said in other places, true nobility is not about being better than someone else, it's about being better than we used to be. Every single experience in my life, right up to this day, was something I needed to go through in order to get to be here now, writing these words. What proof can I offer for this assertion? It happened—that's all the proof I need.

As we look back on our life, we've failed at nothing . . . all we've done is produce some results. It's imperative that we send love to those who were hurt by us and forgiveness to ourselves to heal our inner agony. We can then view it all as what we needed to experience in order to get to a higher place. One thing I've learned in my 65 years is that virtually every spiritual advance I've made toward a closer alignment with God energy has been preceded by some kind of fall from grace. Such "mistakes" allow me to write and speak from a more compassionate stance—that is, they always seem to provide me with the energy to propel myself to a higher place. Truly, I bless all of these "failures" because I know I needed to go *there* in order to get *here*.

Be gentle and forgiving with yourself, abandon any and all shame, and refuse to engage in any self-repudiation. Instead, learn from Leo Tolstoy, who said that "the most difficult thing—but an essential one—is to love Life, to love it even while one suffers, because Life is all. Life is God, and to love Life means to love God."

So love every moment of life, especially your blunder-filled past.

Some Suggestions for Putting the Ideas in This Chapter to Work for You

— When you see people you're used to judging as less than perfect, stop in midthought and remember that they share the same God-force as you. Replace judgments of *grossly overweight, dirty, slovenly, disfigured,* or whatever terminology you normally use, with a nonjudgmental thought of pure love, remembering that no one is unappealing to God. Look for opportunities to replace scornful thoughts with loving ones. Trust me—every time you extend love to those who usually receive anything but is a seed of inspiration.

— Forgiving yourself for everything you've felt shame about is highly important. Whatever happened was necessary, so let go of regret and replace your negative feelings with gratitude for what you've learned. If your objective is to be inspired, then you must eradicate your resistance to that magnificent state of being.

After you've forgiven yourself, extend the same courtesy to everyone who you feel mistreated you. There are three people in my life whom I once felt so much anger and hatred toward that I'd get sick to my stomach whenever I thought of them. However, since I've extended love to these individuals, all manner of great things have flowed to me from the world of Spirit.

Practice forgiveness every day. The most difficult or impossible situations are the most essential!

— Keep a list of everything that interests and excites you, no matter how insignificant. Remind yourself that these are indicators or clues that within and around you lie both the talent and the necessary Spirit assistance to bring them into your reality.

— How about taking the time to give the temple in which you reside the ultimate love and respect? Your physical body is sacred space—it's Divine, beautiful, and perfect—yet you can certainly choose to bestow upon it whatever improvements you wish. There are lots of beneficial housekeeping choices you can make: Firm it up, eliminate toxins, even redecorate it, but keep the awareness of your blessed, Divine, perfect body that's capable of anything you desire from the place of being in-Spirit.

— Here's an inspiring thought to keep close to your heart: *Just as you'll never find light by analyzing the darkness, you'll never find your magnificence by analyzing what you believe to be undistinguished about yourself.* Look for opportunities to verify your greatness, and expand your view of yourself as a splendid creation. Whenever a thought of ordinariness pops into your mind, put the brakes on immediately and affirm something like: *I'm a Divine being, a distinct portion of the essence of God.* This silent reminder will do more for your inspiration than a thousand books and a hundred seminars.

* * *

Dr. Abraham Maslow, perhaps the most influential person in my life many years ago, is quoted at the beginning of this chapter as saying: "What is necessary to change a person is to change his awareness of himself." Consider how you might want to follow his advice. You can never be mediocre because you are magnificent in every way. So seek ways to change your awareness of yourself so that you're fully aware of your magnificence and can become receptive to inspiration, your ultimate calling.

CHAPTER 8

INSPIRATION IS SIMPLE

"I have lived long enough to learn how much there is I can really do without. . . . He is nearest to God who needs the fewest things."

— Socrates

FOR A MOMENT, LET'S IMAGINE what it would be like to be fully alive without a physical shell or any of the stuff we need and desire for maintaining life on Earth. We'd have a mental energy that allowed us to move forward or backward, up or down, instantly creating whatever we desired. We'd be free to wallow in an exquisite existence without time or space as we know it. We'd be in a state of pure bliss, in love with everything and everyone. We'd have no duties or bills to tend to, no fear of losing anything, no one judging us, no possessions to insure, no demands on our time, and no goals to achieve.

What we're envisioning is actually the world of Spirit, which we experienced before we came here and will return to when we shed our body (or as William Butler Yeats poetically called it, our "tattered coat upon a stick").

Remember that a central premise of this book is that inspiration is a state of being here now in this material world, while at the same time reconnecting to our spiritual origins. In order to be receptive to inspiration, we need to eliminate the ego clutter that accumulates all too easily for most of us—after all, if we're preoccupied with events and activities that have nothing to do with inspiration, we're unlikely to notice its summons. So in order to achieve a reunion with our ultimate calling, we need to emulate the clear, uncomplicated world of Spirit.

Three Keys to Keeping Life Simple

While the theme of this chapter is that inspiration is simple, this doesn't mean that we should sit around doing nothing, awaiting Spirit's arrival; instead, it means having faith that our spiritual connection flourishes in a life dedicated to joy, love, and peace. If our daily activities are so overwhelming that we don't make these three things our priority, then we're disregarding the value of living a simple life.

Let's now look at each "simple key" in more detail.

Joy

A hectic schedule crammed with nonpurposeful activities precludes an experience of inspiration. For example, when we accept obligatory committee assignments or board appointments, requests to write on subjects that don't inspire us, or invitations to gatherings we don't want to attend, we feel joy draining from our body and spirit.

Our life must be open to Spirit's guidance in order for us to feel inspired. When the calendar becomes frenzied, full of unnecessary turbulence because we've failed to simplify, we won't be able to hear those long-distance calls from our Source . . . and we'll slip into stress, anguish, and even depression. So whatever it takes to feel joy, we simply must act upon it.

Regardless of our current station in life, we have a spiritual contract to make joy our constant companion—so we must learn to make a conscious choice to say no to anything that takes us away from an inspired life. This can be done gently, while clearly showing others that this is how we choose to live. We can start by turning down requests that involve actions that don't correspond with our inner knowing about why we're here.

Even at work, we can find ways to keep ourselves on an inspirational agenda. For example, during my years as a college professor, I recall being asked over and over to partake in activities that didn't correspond with my own inspiration. So I devised a simple solution: I took on more teaching assignments, and in exchange, my colleagues attended curriculum meetings, served on research committees, and wrote building-improvement reports. I consistently listened to my heart, which always demanded joy.

Keep in mind that it's only difficult or impossible to accomplish joy when we engage in resistant vibrational thinking. If we know that we don't have to live a life stuffed with nonjoyful activities, then we can choose the way of inspiration. Opting for joy involves giving ourselves time for play instead of scheduling a workaholic nightmare. *We deserve to feel joy—it's our spiritual calling.* By giving ourselves free time to read, meditate, exercise, and walk in nature, we're inviting the guidance that's waiting patiently to come calling with inspirational messages.

There's also no law requiring us to be at the continual beck and call of our family members. I see no reason to feel anything but joy when we know it's right to choose to do what we're called to do, even when it interferes with another family member's calling. In fact, children benefit by knowing that the business of parenting is to teach them how *not* to lean on their parents. Raising independent kids to find their own inspiration and look for their own joy is important for everyone—we want them to be doing what they're called to do, ultimately for themselves, not for us. We can take great joy in attending their soccer games and recitals and in being with them and their friends—and when we're inspired, we actually *enjoy* their activities. But let's help them to live their joy, and be able to do it with *or without* us there to cheer them on.

The bottom line is that we can simplify life by cutting down on the busywork that keeps us off purpose. We must curtail such activities and listen to Spirit, staying aware of joy and how simple it is to access.

Love

Thoughts or actions that aren't tuned to love will prevent inspiration from getting through to us—we need to remember that we come from a Source of pure love, so a simple life means incorporating that love as one of the three mainstays of our material existence.

This little four-line poem from the *Rubaiyat of Omar Khayyam*, written approximately 1,000 years ago, says so much about staying focused on love:

> *Ah, love! could thou and I with fate conspire*
> *To grasp this sorry scheme of things entire,*
> *Would not we shatter it to bits—and then*
> *Re-mould it nearer to the heart's desire!*

On the fateful day of September 11, 2001, what stuck in my mind were the cell-phone calls made by the people on the ill-fated planes. Every single call was made to a loved one, to connect back in love or to express final words of love. No one called the office or asked their stockbroker for a final appraisal of their financial status, as relationships that weren't love based didn't enter the thoughts of those who knew they were leaving this physical world. Their top priority was to be certain to close out their lives in love: "Tell the kids that I love them." "I love you!" "Give Mom and Dad my love."

Just as love is the priority in the final moments of life, so it must be as we simplify life *now*. We can go toward a clearer life by examining and purifying our relationships with those we love, with ourselves, and with God. What we're looking for are connections that keep us in an energy of love, which is the highest and fastest energy in the Universe.

Love is also incredibly healing, which reminds me of an article I recently read. Called "The Rescuing Hug," it detailed the first week in the life of a set of twins, one of whom wasn't expected to live. The babies were in two separate incubators, but nurse Gayle Kasparian fought hospital rules to place them together in one. When Gayle did so, the healthier of the twins threw an arm over her sister in an endearing embrace—at which point, the weaker baby's heart rate stabilized and her temperature rose to normal.

Even as tiny infants, our spiritually based instincts tell us to love one another. It's such a simple message, yet it's so powerful. If we organize our life around love—for God, for ourselves, for family and friends, for all humankind, and for the environment—we'll remove a lot of the chaos and disorder that defines our life. This is a way to simplify our life, but more than that, it's a way to attract inspiration.

Peace

Isn't our all-time highest priority to live in peace? We come from a place of peace, yet we've somehow gotten farther and farther away from these origins. When we hooked up with ego, we opted for chaos, even though peace was right there for us. And inspiration and being peaceful go hand in hand.

I know that having inner and outer peace is simply crucial for me. I eschew turmoil, conflict, and agitation and remove myself from these noninspiring elements at every opportunity. After all, I can't be the spiritual being I desire to be or live in God-realization when I'm engaged in any form of bedlam.

Somehow I've been directed to maintain the peacefulness I crave by having those "dormant forces" Patanjali spoke about earlier in the book work for me throughout my career. Many people who have a similar semi-celebrity status as myself are surrounded by a long list of people who orchestrate virtually every aspect of their lives. I, however, have chosen a simpler route, and the Universe has responded by sending me a very few individuals who've supported my desire for peace. I'd like to spend the rest of this section discussing each one of them so that you'll have some clear illustrations of how these wonderful people have helped me stay in-Spirit.

— Years ago I realized that I needed help in managing the affairs of my growing enterprise, yet the idea of agents, business managers, advisors, attorneys, accountants, mediators, personal trainers, bodyguards, and any number of people to represent me seemed beyond my tolerance level. Many of those who do what I do even on a smaller scale have a large entourage of attendants for all manner of duties and activities. And I've had these contemporaries complain to me about being burdened with all of their representatives and spending more than they take in to support the services of all these individuals.

This is not my way—in fact, I have *one person* who handles almost all of my requirements. One day while running a training session for a marathon, God sent me the perfect person to handle so many of my upcoming unforeseen pressures and requirements, in the form of a woman who'd left high school in a foreign country to come to America with her two daughters. She doesn't have any fancy degrees or specialized skills, but what she does have is a heart as big as the sky, fierce loyalty, and a willingness to do whatever it takes to learn with on-the-job training.

Originally from Finland (but now a U.S. citizen), Maya Labos is the ultimate definition of a multitasker. In three decades, she's never said, "I can't do that; it's not my job." She manages every request, answers my mail, books all of my talks and my appearances with the media, takes me to and from airports, maintains my personal privacy by deflecting low-energy requests, and deals with the hundreds of appeals I get for endorsements and writing requests. Yet she also handles innumerable tasks, including grocery shopping, vitamin purchasing, office tidying, or bringing clothes to the cleaners—I can count on her to take care of everything and anything I need.

When I met Maya almost 30 years ago, she was completely broke; today she owns her own home by the ocean and is my best friend, confidante, and associate. You see, when we're open to matching up our desire for peace and simplicity with the peace and simplicity from which we originated, God sends what we need. In my case, I got an "entourage of one" to handle what myriad "specialists" can't do for so many of my contemporaries.

— Every writer needs an editor. Almost 30 years ago, God saw this and sent one to me in the form of the enormously well-read and competent Joanna Pyle. She's been my one and only editorial person for the 25 books I've written; I don't submit to editorial boards. Joanna does for me what many writers ask for from their team of editors, editorial assistants, line editors, rewriters, revisers, amenders, annotators, and so on. I want to keep it simple, and Joanna knows how I write. She's also the only person who can read my scribbles, since I write in longhand.

As the computer age dawned on the publishing world, Joanna trained herself to meet these newly emerging technological requirements—she didn't ask me to write on a computer or to change anything. She knows my desire for simplicity and peace, and she accommodates me perfectly. When I finish a chapter, I send it to Joanna with complete trust that she'll edit it in such a manner that it will be consistent with my original intent. She transcribes it, types it, reorganizes it, and computerizes it—all with a smile and genuine gratitude for being able to fulfill her purpose. Joanna is me; I am Joanna. Once I was able to convince her to leave her nonfulfilling employment as a flight attendant and pursue her bliss as an editor full-time, she was finally able to feel the joy and peace that comes from matching up her energy with her desires. She lives inspiration, and she allows me to do the same.

— I only employ one individual who handles any and all matters related to the complexities of taxes, particularly where foreign royalties are concerned. I don't use a team of legal experts who charge by the hour, or tax consultants who receive as much as what I owe the government. One man, Bob Adelson, knows my desire for peace by keeping it simple, so he organizes everything for me. He works diligently and thoroughly, doing what he loves, and I treasure his presence in my life.

— In 1976, after *Your Erroneous Zones* was published, I decided to move from New York to Florida. I knew absolutely no one in my new hometown, yet I needed an investment person whom I could trust to help me with the bonuses I'd received from the success of my first book. Having been a teacher and university professor before this point, with no experience in (or money for) investing, I knew practically nothing about this world. While contemplating how to start an investment portfolio, I pulled into a gas station, filled my tank, and drove away without realizing that my wallet, which contained $800 in cash, had fallen out of the car and was lying next to the pump.

Just a few hours later, a man called to tell me that he'd found my wallet—including the cash. I went to meet John Darling, who was my angel sent from God to take care of all of my investments for the next 29 years (and he continues to be one of my very best friends and confidants). When I needed someone I could trust, the Universe sent me a stranger who returned my $800 . . . and I've never had a moment of nonpeace regarding investments in the past three decades. John has managed it all for me—always keeping in mind how I like things to be simple, risk free, and uncomplicated— knowing what my ultimate investment objectives were and what I desired for my family.

— I left a large, prestigious New York publishing firm to work with Hay House, mainly because everything in the Big Apple was becoming way too complex. My former publisher employed wonderful people, but the company was too big—it had too many tentacles, too many unkept promises, and too many departments that weren't in harmony with each other (or with me). I felt that too often I was being told, "It's not our fault. The fault is over there in finance or over there in marketing or over there in distribution." It was like a 20-headed monster.

I voted once again for tranquility and simplicity, and once again God sent me a gift—this time in the form of the president and CEO of Louise Hay's publishing company, Hay House. When I met Reid Tracy, we clicked almost immediately. This man—who's unafraid to roll up his sleeves and unload trucks, even though he's in an executive position—promised me personal attention, and he delivered. We talked every day about a publishing company that didn't get so big that it forgot to care for its authors. Reid promised me no large conglomerates and said, "If you have a desire, make it known to me, and I'll act on it." I loved the lack of complications, since I didn't wish to be in a large-business labyrinth any longer. *Simplify, simplify, simplify!*

It has been a glorious experience for both Reid (whom I now consider one of my closest friends) and myself. I wanted peace as a writer, and Louise Hay, whom I've long admired, and her fine president have allowed me to create in peace.

As you can see, I've chosen to allow the world of Spirit to send me those individuals who have helped, rather than hindered, me. Without these fine people and their treasured friendship, I wouldn't be able to be here in Maui, playing tennis and walking on the beach. But mostly I'm able to write from my heart and do it in peaceful ease, knowing that the Universe has taken care of all the details in its own Divine way. When *you* desire peace, simplicity, and honesty and send out a matching vibration to those desires, all I can say is, "Start watching. It's on its way!"

The 12-Step Program to Simplicity

This chapter is going to end a little differently. Rather than giving you some general suggestions for implementing the ideas herein, I'm going to give you 12 very specific tools for simplifying your life. Begin using them today if you're serious about hearing that ultimate call to inspiration.

1. Unclutter your life. You'll feel a real rush of inspiration when you clear out stuff that's no longer useful in your life:

- If you haven't worn it in the past year or two, recycle it for others to use.

- Get rid of old files that take up space and are seldom, if ever, needed.

- Donate unused toys, tools, books, bicycles, and dishes to a charitable organization.

Get rid of anything that keeps you mired in acquisitions that contribute to a cluttered life. In the words of Socrates, "He is nearest to God who needs the fewest things." So the less you need to insure, protect, dust, reorganize, and move, the closer you'll be to hearing inspiration's call.

2. Clear your calendar of unwanted and unnecessary activities and obligations. If you're unavailable for Spirit, you're unlikely to know the glow of inspiration. Had I not been free enough to go running each day back in the 1970s, no Maya. Had I not moved away from the frenetic rush of New York to Florida (where I longed to be), no John. Had I spent all my time on a demanding board, no Joanna. God will indeed work with you and send you the guidance—and the people—you need, but if you're grossly overscheduled, you're going to miss these life-altering gifts. So practice saying no to excessive demands and don't feel guilty about injecting a dose of leisure time into your daily routine.

3. Be sure to keep your free time _free_. Be on the lookout for invitations to functions that may keep you on top of society's pyramid, but that inhibit your access to joyful inspiration. If cocktail parties, social get-togethers, fund-raising events, or even drinking-and-gossiping gatherings with friends aren't really how you want to spend your free time, then don't. Begin declining invitations that don't activate feelings of inspiration.

I find that an evening spent reading or writing letters, watching a movie with a loved one, having dinner with my children, or even exercising alone is far more inspiring than getting dressed to attend a function often filled with small talk. I've learned to be unavailable for such events without apologizing, and consequently have more inspired moments freed up.

4. Take time for meditation and yoga. Give yourself at least 20 minutes a day to sit quietly and make conscious contact with God. I've written an entire book on this subject called *Getting in the Gap,* so I won't belabor it here. I will say that I've received thousands of messages (including the one from Gail Beale, which I shared with you in Chapter 5) from people all over the world, who have expressed their appreciation for learning how to simplify their life by taking the time to meditate.

I also encourage you to find a yoga center near you and begin a regular practice. The rewards are so powerful: You'll feel healthier, less stressed, and inspired by what you'll be able to do with and for your body in a very short time.

5. Return to the simplicity of nature. There's nothing more awe inspiring than nature itself. The fantasy to return to a less tumultuous life almost always involves living in the splendor of the mountains, the forests, or the tundra; on an island; near the ocean; or beside a lake. These are universal urges, since nature is created by the same Source as we are, and we're made up of the same chemicals as all of nature (we're stardust, remember?).

Your urge to simplify and feel inspired is fueled by the desire to be your natural self—that is, your *nature* self. So give yourself permission to get away to trek or camp in the woods; swim in a river, lake, or ocean; sit by an open fire; ride horseback through trails; or ski down a mountain slope. This doesn't have to mean long, planned vacations that are months away—no matter where you live, you're only a few hours or even moments away from a park, campground, or trail that will allow you to enjoy a feeling of being connected to the entire Universe.

6. Put distance between you and your critics. Choose to align yourself with people who are like-minded in their search for simplified inspiration. Give those who find fault or who are confrontational a silent blessing and remove yourself from their energy as quickly as possible. Your life is simplified enormously when you don't have to defend yourself to anyone, and when you receive support rather than criticism. You don't have to endure the criticism with anything other than a polite thank-you and a promise to consider what's been said—anything else is a state of conflict that erases the possibility of your feeling inspired. You never need to defend yourself or your desires to anyone, as those inner feelings are Spirit speaking to you. Those thoughts are sacred, so don't ever let anyone trample on them.

7. Take some time for your health. Consider that the number one health problem in America seems to be obesity. How can you feel inspired and live in simplicity if you're gorging on excessive amounts of food and eliminating the exercise that the body craves? Recall that your body is a sacred temple where you reside for this lifetime, so make some time every single day for exercising it. Even if you can only manage a walk around the block, just do it. Similarly, keep the words *portion control* uppermost in your consciousness—your stomach is the size of your fist, not a wheelbarrow! Respect your sacred temple *and* simplify your life by being an exerciser and a sensible eater. I promise that you'll feel inspired if you act on this today!

8. Play, play, play! You'll simplify your life and feel inspired if you learn to play rather than work your way through life. I love to be around kids because they inspire me with their laughter and frivolity. In fact, if I've heard it once, I've heard it a thousand times: "Wayne, you've never grown up—you're always playing." I take great pride in this! I play onstage when I speak, and I'm playing now as I write.

Many years ago I was given a tremendous opportunity to appear on *The Tonight Show* with Johnny Carson. The man who took a chance on me, booking me even though I was an unknown at the time, was a talent coordinator named Howard Papush. It was my first big break, and I went on to appear on that show 36 additional times.

Now it's my turn to say thank you to Howard. He's written a wonderful book titled *When's Recess? Playing Your Way Through the Stresses of Life,* which I encourage you to read. (Howard also conducts workshops that teach people how to play and have fun in life.) In the book, Howard shares this great quote from Richard Bach: "You are led through your lifetime by the inner learning creature, the playful spiritual being that is your real self." I couldn't agree more—by all means, get back in touch with your real, playful self, and take every opportunity to play! Notice how it makes everything so sweet, and so simple.

9. Slow down. One of Gandhi's most illuminating observations reminds us that "there is more to life than increasing its speed." This is great advice for simplifying your life—in fact, slow everything way down for a few moments right here and now. Slowly read these words. Slow your breathing down so that you're aware of each inhalation and exhalation. . . .

When you're in your car, downshift and relax. Slow down your speech, your inner thoughts, and the frantic pace of everything you do. Take more time to hear others. Notice your inclination to interrupt and get the conversation over with, and then choose to listen instead. Stop to enjoy the stars on a clear night and the cloud formations on a crisp day. Sit down in a mall and just observe how everyone seems in a hurry to get nowhere.

By slowing down, you'll simplify and rejoin the perfect pace at which creation works. Imagine trying to hurry nature up by tugging at an emerging tomato plant—you're as natural as that plant, so let yourself be at peace with the perfection of nature's plan.

10. Do everything you can to eschew debt. Remember that you're attempting to simplify your life here, so you don't need to purchase more of what will complicate and clutter your life. If you can't afford it, let it go until you can. By going into debt, you'll just add layers of anxiety onto your life. That anxiety will then take you away from your peace, which is where you are when you're in-Spirit. When you have to work extra hard to pay off debts, the present moments of your life are less enjoyable; consequently, you're further away from the joy and peace that are the trademarks of inspiration. You're far better off to have less and enjoy the days of your life than to take on debt and invite stress and anxiety where peace and tranquility could have reigned. And remember that the money you have in your possession is nothing but energy—so refuse to plug in to an energy system that's not even there.

11. Forget about the cash value. I try not to think about money too frequently because it's been my observation that people who do so tend to think about almost nothing else. So do what your heart tells you will bring you joy, rather than determining whether it will be cost-effective. If you'd really enjoy that whale-watching trip, for instance, make the decision to do so—don't deny yourself the pleasures of life because of some monetary detail. Don't base your purchases on getting a discount, and don't rob yourself of a simple joy because you didn't get a break on the price. You can afford a happy, fulfilling life, and if you're busy right now thinking that I have some nerve telling you this because of your bleak financial picture, then you have your own barrier of resistance.

Make an attempt to free yourself from placing a price tag on everything you have and do—after all, in the world of Spirit, there are no price tags. Don't make money the guiding principle for what you have or do; rather, simplify your life and return to Spirit by finding the inherent value in everything. A dollar does not determine worth, even though you live in a world that attempts to convince you otherwise.

12. Remember *your* spirit. When life tends to get too complex, too fast, too cluttered, too deadline oriented, or too type A for you, stop and remember your own spirit. You're headed for inspiration, a simple, peaceful place where you're in harmony with the perfect timing of all creation. Go there in your mind, and stop frequently to remember what you really want.

* * *

A man who personified success at the highest intellectual and social levels would hardly seem one to quote on simplifying our life, yet here's what Albert Einstein offers us on this subject: "Possessions, outward success, publicity, luxury—to me these have always been contemptible. I believe that a simple and unassuming manner of life is best for everyone, best both for the body and the mind."

Wow! I'd say this is pretty good advice, wouldn't you?

CHAPTER 9

THERE'S NOTHING MORE POWERFUL THAN AN IDEA WHOSE TIME HAS COME

" . . . neither does anyone, however many wounds he may have received, die, unless he has run his allotted term of life: nor does any man, though he sits quietly by the fireside under his own roof, escape the more his fated doom."

— AESCHYLUS

INSPIRATION REQUIRES FAITH—after all, returning to Spirit while in our physical body is unlikely to be successful if we don't believe that it's possible. We may even have to focus on renewing our faith prior to accessing inspiration, since faith allows us to trust and thereby make use of the vast power that's responsible for creating every physical object in the Universe.

Faith is an internal knowing that the All-Creating Spirit provides what we need precisely on schedule. This doesn't mean that we don't have a voice in what happens to us—we do, but the voice only becomes activated when we get our ego out of the way and realign with Spirit. When our spirit works with the Divine Spirit, we can participate in creation and truly know the meaning of this chapter's title, "There's Nothing More Powerful Than an Idea Whose Time Has Come."

There's perfect timing in the Universe, and our arrival on Earth was a part of that synchronicity. In other words, *we* were an idea of God's whose time had come. This chapter introduces the concept of perfect timing and how to believe in it, notice it, tune in to it, and apply it.

Faith Banishes All Doubt

We know that ego has virtually no control over what happens to us: Our body grows, develops, changes, and declines independent of ego's desires or opinions. We know that eventually we'll shed this garment we've been wearing for a lifetime—not when our ego decides, but when that idea's time has come. Reread the Aeschylus quote at the beginning of this chapter about our "allotted term of life" as an example of what I'm referring to.

Aeschylus was the most famous playwright and scholar of his era, and he claimed direct Divine guidance in his writing. (He was also a contemporary of Socrates, Lao-tzu, Zoroaster, Buddha, and Confucius, who all lived during the 5th century B.C. It's intriguing to note how many visionaries were on the planet simultaneously!) Basically, he tells us that the shape of life must run its allotted course and that we're here to do what Spirit intends. According to Aeschylus, we'll leave Earth and shake off our physical body in concert with Spirit's plan for us. Whether we're ready at age 17, 25, or 105, he advises us to trust in our Source. (I add to this message that at whatever age we read these words, it's the right time to realize that we're in the process of surrendering to Spirit for the remaining portion of our allotment.)

The question now becomes: Can we join with Spirit and play a decisive role in what ideas, happenings, events, or people will show up for us? The answer is a resounding *yes!* Recall once again those words of Patanjali that I shared in the opening chapters: "When you are inspired . . . dormant forces, faculties, and talents become alive." This is where faith becomes critically important.

You see, we must have faith in a Universe that's created and guided by an intelligence greater than our ego—one where there can be no accidents. When an idea's time has come, it can't be stopped—but by raising our vibration to match that of the Universal Source of Being, we can bring about that idea's time. We can raise our level of consciousness from ego and group dominance to what I call "visionary consciousness," in which we reconnect to the mind of God. We banish all doubt by our *knowing,* which is a higher level of consciousness than *believing.* Our vision is God's vision, in a manner of speaking. Let me offer you an example of how this visionary consciousness plays out.

One of my greatest teachers—and a man I now call my friend—is Ram Dass. He lives from the spiritual faith I'm writing about, without doubts or fears. I'd been a long-distance follower and devotee of his for 30 years, always knowing that we'd connect in person. I had this knowing without ever needing to hurry or force what I sensed was a future connection in his and my lifetime. And when that idea's time came, Ram Dass moved to Maui, where I'm writing to you from right now.

Today I have the great pleasure of being in the service of my teacher, helping him in these advanced years of his life. The following self-explanatory letter that I wrote recently is posted on my Website, **www.drwaynedyer.com.** I'm including it here to precisely illustrate how what I'm relating in this chapter can unfold.

> One of the truly great men of our time needs our help, and I write these words to encourage your generosity and support. Back in the 1960s a Harvard professor named Richard Alpert left behind the hectic world of academia and traveled to India—there he was to meet his spiritual teacher, who gave him a new purpose to fulfill along with a new name. He, of course, is Ram Dass.
>
> His guru told him to love everyone, feed people, and see God everywhere. Ram Dass became a person who lived out this mandate, doing what so many of us could only dream. He connected to his spirit and devoted his life to serving others.
>
> In 1969 he wrote and published the signature book on spirituality and applied higher awareness, *Be Here Now.* In keeping with his commitment to love everyone and feed people, he donated all of the royalties and profits to foundations that did just that. With millions of dollars at stake, Ram Dass simply chose to live his life as a man of service to God.
>
> After years spent in India in pursuit of a higher, more enlightened consciousness for himself and for our troubled world,

he returned to the United States to lecture throughout the country. He spoke to packed venues wherever he went; and, as always, he donated the proceeds to such causes as would keep him in harmony with his mandate to serve. He cofounded the Seva Foundation (**www.seva.org**), and his writing and lecture fees were primary sources for this compassionate and inspired work.

To me, Ram Dass was and is the finest speaker I have ever heard, period! He was my role model onstage; always gentle and kind; always speaking (without notes) from his heart, sharing his inspiring stories; and always with great humor. I tell you this from my own heart: I could listen to his lectures for hours and always felt saddened when they would end. He was the voice for Applied Spirituality—his life was the model. When he was threatened by having his own private sexual preference exposed, in a time when a closet was the only place that was even mildly safe, Ram Dass called a press conference and proudly announced his preference to the world. He paved the way for tolerance and love when no one else would dare to do so.

Most of us could only dream of defying the conventional life and living out our inner callings to promote a cause that was bigger than our own lives—to leave the security of a guaranteed career and a country where comfort was ensured—all to live in a foreign land with few conveniences, traveling and meditating for a more peaceful world. It is what Saint Francis did in the 13th century, and what Ram Dass did in our lifetime.

When Ram Dass's father, who had largely criticized his son's unconventional lifestyle, was close to death, Ram Dass devoted himself to 100 percent service in those final years. He fed his father, he bathed his father, he placed him on and off the toilet until the day he died. Why? Because he felt this was his mandate. He wanted to experience true service on a 24/7 basis and know firsthand the joy that comes from giving one's own life away in the service of others. Always, for over 30 years, Ram Dass was in the service of others.

In 1997 Ram Dass was struck by a semiparalyzing stroke and became wheelchair bound. Still he wrote of his adventure in a powerful book titled *Still Here*. He continued to travel, although he could no longer walk, and continued to speak to audiences, although he spoke from a slowed-down body—but still, he did it to serve others.

Now it is our turn. . . . Ram Dass's body can no longer endure the rigors of travel. He has come to Maui, where I live and write. I speak with him frequently and am often humbled by the tears in his beautiful 73-year-old eyes as he apologizes for not having prepared for his own elderly health care—for what he now perceives as burdensome to others. He still intends to write and teach, however, without the travel—we can now come to him. Maui is healing—Maui is where Ram Dass wishes to stay for now.

He is currently living in a home on Maui, which he doesn't own and is in jeopardy of losing. I am asking all of you to help purchase this home and to set up a financial foundation to take care of this man who has raised so much money to ensure the futures of so many others—to live out what Ram Dass has practiced with his actions. Please be generous and prompt—no one is more deserving of our love and financial support. In the end, these donations will help ensure that Ram Dass and his work will reach another generation or remind a current generation that it is in giving that we receive.

If there has ever been a great spirit who lived in our lifetime, literally devoting his life to the highest principles of Spirit, it has been Ram Dass. I love this man; he has been my inspiration, and the inspiration for millions of us. It is now time to show him how we feel by doing what he has taught all of us to do—just be here for him, now.

Please send your donations to: Ram Dass, c/o Hay House, P. O. Box 5100, Carlsbad, CA 92018-5100.

In love and light,

Wayne W. Dyer

Truly, giving is receiving and vice versa. Ram Dass lived a life of giving; by staying in-Spirit, I was sent to this man who has meant so much to me. I always had a knowing that I'd be involved in his mission and his life—it was an idea that I held in-Spirit for several decades, and now its time has come and cannot be stopped. (If you feel called to help, you can send in any contribution to the address above, and I will see that it goes directly to Ram Dass.)

It was Ram Dass's total belief in what his spiritual teacher told him to do with his life that allowed this all to unfold. When we banish all doubt in favor of faith, there's nothing more powerful on this planet. You must believe, and then you'll see it unfolding right before your eyes.

Spirit's Timing at Work

The power of an idea whose time has come is really the power of Spirit at work. Equality for all is how God is, for instance, and we seek to be like God. When enough of us, along with one or two at visionary consciousness, begin to contemplate these in-Spirit ideas, they can't be stopped. Let's take some time here to note a few such ideas from America's history:

— When it was time for the unspeakably horrid practice of slavery to be abolished, that was an idea whose time had come. This was because a critical mass of individuals with a new vision for humanity began to contemplate something that had been espoused a few generations earlier: "We hold these truths to be self-evident, that all men are created equal." It took more than 85 years after Thomas Jefferson wrote these words, but then the idea couldn't be stopped—even though slaves represented a tiny part of the population and had no voting rights. When a man with visionary consciousness, Abraham Lincoln (along with many others), approached this idea from an inspirational perspective, it was clear that the time had indeed come to end slavery. This new idea of equality for all is the way of Spirit.

— We can see also an idea whose time had come in the granting of voting rights for women in 1920. Despite the opposition of a nonvisionary President (Woodrow Wilson), and over the objection of a majority of men who had voting privileges, the idea couldn't be stopped. Several visionary women, who aligned with many other men and women, believed and made it happen—a right that we take for granted today.

— The racial integration of the United States is another example of an idea whose time had come. When this concept began to surface in the visionary consciousness of a few individuals such as John F. Kennedy; Martin Luther King, Jr.; Lyndon Johnson; and Rosa Parks; it couldn't be stopped—despite the objections of millions of people, many of whom were in positions of political power. Today, in schools that once practiced segregation, we have a multiracial student body. Racial integration is still in the process of manifesting everywhere in our society, and there's much still to be done, but make no mistake about it, this idea cannot be stopped.

— Gay rights is another idea whose time has come. One of the many reasons I admire Ram Dass so much is the stand he took a long time ago on equal rights for people of all sexual orientations. No individual or group can be denied legal or social privileges because we all come from one Source, which excludes no one. An idea whose time has come is always in perfect alignment with our originating Spirit.

— Finally, the shift in consciousness from a collective belief that smoking in public places is permissible to one where it's not tolerated was an idea whose time had come. The idea became unstoppable when one visionary airline banned smoking on their commercial flights—and then the rest fell into spiritual alignment. Since we come from a nontoxic Source of Well-Being, aligning with It is our destiny and can't be stopped.

I could go on and on with examples of such ideas manifesting in our society, but instead I propose that we begin looking around us for evidence of ideas whose time has come. You see, when we're ready, willing, and open to it, the Divine guidance we seek will spring into action on our behalf. It has been that way throughout our life. For example, the people we've had love affairs with—regardless of how long the relationships lasted—are all characters in this dream of ours called "life." They come to us for any number of reasons, such as to help us create a child (or children), to teach us forgiveness, or to assist us in fulfilling some other destiny.

It's difficult for our ego to grasp, but every single person who's drifted in and out of our life is a part of our Divinely chosen life experience—that is, they are ideas whose time had come. As we move into a life of inspiration, we'll find it easy and even necessary to give thanks for all of these individuals, and to take serious note of what they brought us at the time of their arrival and/or departure.

By the same token, when we needed to have a certain vocational experience, it was made available to us. Because we were a vibrational match to what showed up, we took it in and got out of it precisely what we needed. And when we were no longer a vibrational match to that job, those people, that city, that house, or whatever, we left.

We're in a system that's directed by a Supreme Intelligence, and we're a part of that system. *Everything is on purpose.* Our vibrational matchup determines what we attract and what we repel in our life. We needn't focus on what's already happened and what we've gone through; rather, we must shift our vibration upward so that it harmonizes with Spirit, and then—and only then—will spiritually based ideas come knocking on our door. These ideas won't give up or go away because, as we know, there's nothing in this Universe more powerful than an idea whose time has come. Our responsibility is simply to become beings who expect and await inspired ideas that will not and cannot be stopped.

Manifesting in-Spirit Ideas

Our expectations are virtual ideas that are manifesting right now in our life. Remember that we receive what we match up with energetically, so if we persist in expecting our ideas to work, we'll create an idea whose time has come. It's our job to shift the energy of our thoughts so that they harmonize with what it is that we truly wish to attract.

For example, many years ago I believed in something called "writer's block," those times when ideas simply refused to flow. Today I have a very different point of view: I know that in some way, God writes all the books and builds all the bridges. Now when

I sit down to write, I expect ideas to flow through me and onto the pages. I feel as if I'm a vibrational match to ideas that want to be expressed in the words I write; consequently, I know that these are ideas whose time has come—they're matching up with me right here, right now, and they can't be stopped.

If I ask myself, "Where does what appears on this paper really come from?" I know that I don't own them. The words flow from Spirit to physical manifestation because I allow myself to be a receiving agent who's willing to transcribe them on pieces of paper that will eventually be a book. I expect these ideas to be here and know that they can't be stopped. I sit here awestruck and in a state of love and gratitude for being able to be used in such an inspirational way—while writing about inspiration, no less!

The crucial message here is to *match our desires to our expectations.* We need to see it all arriving and know that it can't be stopped. We must learn to smile inwardly at those who scoff at our optimism and then go on about the business of expecting our in-Spirit ideas to manifest by looking for evidence of their arrival. At the slightest hint of their appearance, we can energize them with gratitude.

Finding even a penny can be a clue that our expectation of abundance is manifesting. That penny is right where it belongs, so we should treat it like a treasure-hunt clue. That is, we should gratefully assume that it was placed there for us to shift our expectations so that they're compatible with the unlimited abundance that we desire. We can say, "Thank you, God, for this symbol of abundance," knowing that we've initiated a new idea that's so powerful that its time has come!

We need to create compatibility with Spirit by changing around our expectations so that they align with the central premise of this chapter: *There's nothing more powerful than an idea whose time has come.* Try these words out as personal affirmations for tuning in to this new expectation: *I desire it. It's on its way. There's nothing for me to worry about.* Whatever "it" is—a job, a promotion, financing, the right person, well-being, the return to health, information, or what have you, tell yourself: *It's an idea that can't be stopped because I'm balanced perfectly with my Source of Being. I am at God-realization, and with God all things are possible, so that leaves nothing out.*

We don't want to ask the Universe to be different so that we can feel better, but we can *choose* to feel better by shifting our expectations so that we're vibrating with the Universe. We don't have to be like anyone else in order to achieve this vibrational harmony because we're individualized expressions of God, unique in what we have and what we desire. After all, when we approach a long food buffet, we don't focus on eliminating the things we don't want; instead, we begin to vibrate in our thoughts to what we *do* want and ignore what we don't.

Keep in mind that our expectations are uniquely our own. They're ideas whose time has come . . . and that have always been coming.

Oneness and Sameness

I'd like to take a minute here to explain that there's a vast difference between oneness and sameness. We're all one, but we're *not* the same. If this sounds like a conflict, think about the fact that there's only one light, yet there are many colors; there's only one fire, yet there are many bonfires; and there's only one water, yet there are many lakes, rivers, and oceans. Likewise, although we all come from one Source, we are individualized expressions of It, and therefore unique.

We live in a society that often seeks to make us conform and fit in with everybody else, yet Spirit created each of us as a distinct, separate entity that's unique in all of creation. Thus, in order to be inspired, we must maintain our singular individuality while seeing our connection to our Source and to everyone and everything in the Universe. Each of us is an unparalleled idea whose time had come: We didn't manifest to be the same as each other, but to be like God and express ourselves as we agreed to when we merged into physical form.

I've always loved author Leo Buscaglia, and here's a story he often told that perfectly illustrates the point I'm making.

The animals got together in the forest one day and decided to start a school. There was a rabbit, a bird, a squirrel, a fish and an eel, and they formed a Board of Education. The rabbit insisted that running be in the curriculum. The bird insisted that flying be in the curriculum. The fish insisted that swimming be in the curriculum, and the squirrel insisted that perpendicular tree climbing be in the curriculum. They put all of these things together and wrote a Curriculum Guide. Then they insisted that *all* of the animals take *all* of the subjects. Although the rabbit was getting an A in running, perpendicular tree climbing was a real problem for him; he kept falling over backwards. Pretty soon he got to be sort of brain damaged, and he couldn't run anymore. He found that instead of making an A in running, he was making a C and, of course, he always made an F in perpendicular climbing. The bird was really beautiful at flying, but when it came to burrowing in the ground, he couldn't do so well. He kept breaking his beak and wings. Pretty soon he was making a C in flying as well as an F in burrowing, and he had a hellava time with perpendicular tree climbing. The moral of the story is that the person who was valedictorian of the class was a mentally retarded eel who did everything in a halfway fashion. But the educators were all happy because everybody was taking all of the subjects, and it was called a broad-based education.

Respect your oneness and eschew any pressure to be a conformist—be the being you came here to be. After all, *you* are that powerful idea whose time has come.

Some Suggestions for Putting the Ideas in This Chapter to Work for You

— Become aware of as many things that impinge on your reality as you can, particularly the ones you call "meaningless" or "circumstantial." *Nothing* is meaningless in this Universe, so remind yourself that whatever shows up in your life has been attracted there. For example, an accident isn't any kind of karmic payback or something to feel guilty about—it simply means that you were a match to it. When you stub your toe, bang your elbow, cut your hand, feel a twinge, get a headache, or anything similar, remind yourself that this is energy that has shown up on time. Try to notice what you were thinking at that precise moment, and be open to the idea that it showed up physically to teach you something.

— *You get what you think about, whether you want it or not! So be careful about what you think about.* Memorize this beautiful little homily and post it in a conspicuous place in your home or workplace. Always be mindful of your thoughts about what you expect from the Universe.

— Send a silent blessing to everyone who's ever shown up, or continues to show up, in your life. A surly waiter can trigger a reminder to send love out if that's what you want back. An ex-spouse can be blessed for what he or she offered you, and even for being an ex. A slow driver ahead of you is an idea of God who's shown up on time—bless him for giving you an opportunity to slow down, thus saving you from the speeding ticket you were a vibrational match to before he showed up.

— Resist fitting in: Do it gently, but do it just the same. Every time someone attempts to get you to conform, affirm: *I am an individualized expression of God.* That's all you need to remember. Then be in the place within yourself where you feel one with God, and send love to those who'd push you in the direction of uniformity and conventionality. Refuse to be "a mentally retarded eel who [does] everything in a halfway fashion," or even worse, the way other people want you to.

— Most important, *have faith.* Trust in a Universe that's endless and endlessly creating. Trust that the Creative Source of All knows exactly what It's doing. Trust in the awareness that there can't be accidents in such an intelligent system. Look out at the vastness of the Universe and contemplate the power of its Source—by doing so, you'll shift your energy. Practice this every day.

* * *

Truly, there's absolutely nothing in this Universe, including ourselves, that isn't perfectly timed. There are no wrongful deaths or mistakes—what shows up is ours, and it showed up precisely on schedule. Before we move on to Part III, I'd like you to think about the simple wisdom that the former slave and philosopher Epictetus imparted to us nearly 2,000 years ago: "It is my business to manage carefully and dexterously whatever happens." Now there's a powerful idea whose time has come!

PART III

GIVING AND
RECEIVING
INSPIRATION

*"We ought, so far as it lies within our power,
to aspire to immortality, and do all that we can
to live in conformity with the highest that is within us;
for even if it is small in quantity, in power
and preciousness, it far excels all the rest."*

— ARISTOTLE

CHAPTER 10

ABSORBING
THE INSPIRATION
OF OTHERS

*"A man may have never entered a church or a mosque,
nor performed any ceremony; but if he realizes God
within himself, and is thereby lifted above the vanities
of the world, that man is a holy man, a saint,
call him what you will . . ."*

— VIVEKANANDA

ONE OF THE BEST MEANS AVAILABLE for heeding our
ultimate calling comes from connecting to the saints that the
Indian monk Vivekananda referred to more than 100 years ago.
The holy people mentioned in this context don't necessarily need
to be connected to a religious practice; in fact, it's unlikely that
they'll be dressed in devotional garments or engaged in any theological studies at all. Rather, those we view as inspirational will
be the ones who radiate spiritual energy back to us and fit Vivekananda's brilliant observation. They've reached a higher level of
God-realization than most, suspended their ego, and have lived
from a high-energy perspective. They're spiritual beings having a
human experience, rather than the other way around.

One of the things we absolutely know about energy is that
when higher/faster energy comes in contact with lower vibrations,
they're converted into higher energy. Thus, light introduced into

a dark room not only eliminates the darkness, but converts that darkness to light as well. (If this concept intrigues you, I suggest that you read my books *There's a Spiritual Solution to Every Problem* and *The Power of Intention*.)

The parallel I'm drawing here is that when we enter the energy field of someone who's connected to Spirit, we find ourselves not only forsaking our uninspired ways, but also converting to their higher energy—in other words, we become inspired just by being in their presence. However, identifying those who actually live their lives in-Spirit is often not as simple as it sounds.

What Inspirational People Are <u>Not</u>

It's possible for someone to achieve at a high level, earn many accolades, be widely admired and respected, but not be living from Spirit. Inspirational people aren't necessarily highly motivated in society's sense of the word; after all, such individuals may just be chasing after more symbols of success, satisfying their desire to dominate and control others by acquiring as much power as possible. People who have motivated *us* are also not necessarily inspirational: We may have been motivated by those who threatened or beat us, or cursed and called us a fool and a wimp for not doing what they thought we should be doing. Clearly, inspiration wasn't part of their motivation!

We also can't assume that all teachers are living their ultimate calling. A good instructor might be very knowledgeable about a given subject and extremely effective at conveying that knowledge to students, but he or she might also be very disconnected from God-realization. Teachers often have such low self-esteem that they lose themselves completely in devotion to something that's far removed from their true calling—especially when great teaching skills can fill a void and seem to be a substitute for that calling. Of course I'm not saying that all teachers are lacking in God-realization, but be wary of assuming that a gifted instructor is automatically living in-Spirit.

A person may have the highest intellectual credentials available and still be detached from his or her Spirit. The ability to cite historical sources, speak with distinction, and earn advanced degrees doesn't automatically mean that someone is capable of inspiring others. (Once again, it doesn't disqualify that individual either.) The smartest people may turn us off with their pomposity and braggadocio, or they may be so cerebral that it's difficult to know what they're talking about. Be on the lookout for mistaking intellectualization for inspiration. The journey to our ultimate calling isn't a scholastic endeavor—there are no written exams, no grades to earn, no report cards, and no advanced degrees.

It's important to understand that any of the traditional measures of success, such as job promotions, wealth, public acclaim, expensive clothing, a commanding presence, verbal adeptness, a voluminous vocabulary, a charismatic appearance, fame, and so forth don't necessarily mean high marks as an inspirational person. In fact, some people who rate very high marks on the ego-based indexes of success are the ones I find most difficult to be around—and totally uninspiring.

While fame in all of its forms seems highly desirable and is focused upon by endless television shows discussing the personal lives of those who are in the news (particularly show business), this does not measure the ability to inspire in the slightest. When one of my daughters once told me that her goal was to become famous, I urged her to shift her sights to living and acting in rapport with her passion and then letting the fame thing take care of itself.

I've met many celebrities in all fields of endeavor, and I can assure you that public notoriety is not in any way an indicator of a person's connection to Spirit. And if I happen to be famous personally, it's not because I chose it or even earned it. Fame is located outside of me—it's in the opinions that others have of me. It's my choice to be inspired, however, and that always involves being independent of the opinions of others.

Inspirational people aren't interested in winning a popularity contest, especially when those who seek praise and recognition often do so to soothe feelings of insecurity. In general, people who doubt their Divinity fear being criticized because they see themselves as fraudulent beings; consequently, they take on the full-time job of trying to be liked by everyone they meet. Despite their obvious popularity, they'd be disastrous in the inspiration department.

I need to add a disclaimer here: I don't in any way want to imply that a person who *has* gained great popularity and notoriety is thereby disqualified from being a source of inspiration. Quite the contrary: Many of the most inspiring people I've come across in my life have achieved worldwide acclaim. I simply urge you not to equate inspiration with recognition.

What Inspirational People <u>Are</u>

Now let's take a look at the qualities we *do* find in inspirational people—that is, those special individuals who've risen above their ego and the vanities of the world—and how our awareness of, and association with, them helps raise our vibrations to the level of Spirit.

Over the years, as a result of teaching at a major university and lecturing to audiences of experts, I've had the distinct pleasure of being in the company of some extremely knowledgeable people. I've also been blessed to associate with a number of very wise individuals who have achieved enlightened mastery in their own lives and as spiritual teachers. My observation is that the more expertise so-called experts appear to have, the less joy they seem to experience, while those who are genuinely wise consistently have an aura of joy that permeates their being and radiates outward, impacting those around them.

We can use this "joy index" as a nonscientific measure of inspiration. When we meet others who we think might be living in-Spirit, we must ask the following questions: Do they seem to have a rapturous heart, sending out signals that they love the world and everyone in it? Are they jubilant about the work they do? Do they see the world as a friendly place? Are they at peace with themselves?

Do they appear to be kind rather than judgmental? Are they confident without being boorish? Do they tend to be cheerful? Do they love to play? Are they elated to be in the company of young children as well as older people? Do they listen rather than lecture? Are they willing to be students as well as teachers? Do they love nature? Are they in awe of the world? Do they express rational humility? Are they approachable? Do they take great pleasure in serving others? Do they seem to have tamed their ego? Do they accept all people as equals? Are they open to new ideas? The answers to these questions will help us ascertain whether another person is potentially an inspiring influence in our life.

Those who have the gift of inspiration exude something that's difficult to pin down intellectually, yet is undeniably recognizable in how we feel in their presence: We can sense that they're aligned with the Source Energy from which we all originate. We perceive a place within them that resonates deeply within ourselves—a vibrational recognition of inspiration—and they have much to offer us. We recognize their high spiritual energy, which longs to be active in our life. When we feel this resonance, it's reflected in a feeling that's similar to a warm, soothing shower that's running deep within us.

When I'm in the presence of an inspiring person, the first thing I notice is this warm shower overtaking me: It's like a wave of energy that slowly moves down my shoulders and spine, and I know something is happening energetically. Even though I can't see, touch, smell, or hear it, I know that I'm experiencing a shift that makes me feel incredibly good (or, as I think of it, *incredibly God*).

My Experiences with Inspiring People

In this section, I'd like to further illustrate what inspirational people *are* by noting some individuals who have particularly impacted my life with their high energy.

— I vividly recall the days of the Cuban missile crisis more than 40 years ago. I'd recently been discharged from active duty in the Navy after four years and was attending Wayne State University in Detroit. If the U.S. had been drawn into a war with the U.S.S.R., I would have been at the top of the list to be called back to active duty because I had a top-secret job classification. But more than my concern about my own status was what had us collectively biting our fingernails globally—that is, the thought of the consequences of an exchange of nuclear weapons, which would put all of civilization at risk.

I'll never forget the scene that the film *Thirteen Days* reenacted so well. After being besieged by his military advisors to nuke the entire island of Cuba, and encouraged by others to take alternative decisive action that could easily lead to war, President Kennedy retired alone to his chambers in the White House and reminded himself of what he believed the number one duty of the President was: to keep the country out of war. Having already fought in one war that had also taken the life of his older brother, Joseph, JFK knew how damaging such a battle with the Soviet Union would be, so he retreated in solitude and allowed the peace of Spirit to guide him. Ultimately, the idea for a blockade—and a prayer for a peaceful resolution—took hold of him. He went to Spirit in a time of crisis, and his being in-Spirit rather than "in-ego" turned the tide of history.

President Kennedy was a source of inspiration to me, but not because of his political views or any of his Presidential actions; rather, I embraced him as a man who conveyed love, peace, and joy in his demeanor and showed respect for all people by vowing to end segregation in America. As Robert McNamara, Kennedy's Secretary of Defense, once observed, if JFK had lived, there would have been no Vietnam War. That's because he believed that war should be an absolute last resort, and that his primary job as President was to maintain the peace.

I found JFK inspiring back in the early 1960s, and I've continued to be profoundly touched by his spirit throughout my lifetime. He inspired me!

— In 1978 I was invited to go to Vienna to participate in a presentation to a group of young presidents of companies. I was assigned to be on a panel with a man who had been a huge source of inspiration to me: Viktor Frankl. Frankl was a medical doctor who had been herded off to die in a Nazi concentration camp in WWII; while imprisoned, he kept notes that ultimately became a book called *Man's Search for Meaning.* This work, which touched me deeply many years later, illustrated not only how Dr. Frankl survived the horrors of Auschwitz, but also how he helped other camp mates do the same. For example, he taught his fellow human beings how to find meaning and even joy in a fish head floating in the dirty water that masqueraded as soup. He taught them to be with his spirit and infuse it in others who were giving up on life. He even practiced sending love and peace to his captors, and refused to feel hatred and vengeance because he knew that it was foreign to his spirit, which he wouldn't forsake.

So, 33 years after his liberation, I was about to address hundreds of corporate presidents who were all under the age of 50 (as I was at the time). I'd read *Man's Search for Meaning* as a young doctoral student and practiced Frankl's logotherapy, which taught therapists in training to help clients find meaning in their existence regardless of their circumstances. Viktor Frankl had been one of the truly inspirational figures in my life, and being on the same panel—under the pretext of being a colleague of this master teacher—was overwhelming to me. And an afternoon I've never forgotten followed, full of pure exhilaration and inspiration.

Viktor Frankl stayed true to his spiritual origins in the face of horrors that destroyed so many. When I met him, he exuded joy, peace, kindness, and love, and he wasn't bitter. Instead, he felt that his experience taught him lessons he'd never have known otherwise. I spent a good part of that afternoon in Vienna in 1978 listening and being in awe; and now, years later, I'm still greatly impacted by the presence of this man in my life. Yes, indeed, he inspired me.

131

— In 1994, 24-year-old college student Immaculée Ilibagiza came home to be with her family in Kibuye, Rwanda, for the Easter holidays . . . and inadvertently found herself in the middle of one of the worst genocides in history. As a member of the Tutsi tribe, Immaculée was forced to hide in a tiny bathroom (which was configured in such a way that it appeared to be inaccessible from the house) with seven other women for a total of three terrifying months. As she told me, "By the grace of God, we were never found. How that happened, I do not know. All we could hear was the smoke of hatred coming from the men right outside the door."

After living in this terror for 90 days, trembling in fear every day, knowing that they would be hacked to death if they were discovered, the women were finally released from their entombment into the protection of French soldiers. As Immaculée related: "When we were finally safe, I learned how most of my family had died: My father was shot by soldiers, my mother was killed by machete, and my younger brother was murdered in a stadium while searching for food. My big brother was executed after questioning—they said that they wanted to see the brain of a person who had a master's degree, so they cut him to pieces."

I met this incredible woman in New York after she was granted an asylum visa as a victim of this organized attempt at ethnic cleansing by a band of thugs. (Just about one million men, women, and children were systematically slaughtered with machetes or blunt instruments, and the U.S. didn't intervene—something that former President Clinton publicly acknowledged was the greatest failure of his administration.) Immaculée isn't bitter or filled with rage—she merely wants to be sure that such a tragedy never occurs again. She has love and faith in her heart, and she applied these spiritual gifts to the telling of her story, which has just been published as a remarkable book through Hay House. I felt privileged to have been able to write the Foreword for this amazing work, which is called *Left to Tell: Discovering God Amidst the Rwandan Holocaust.*

I'm honored to join this Divinely inspiring woman by going to Rwanda and helping set up a program to educate and provide for the vast number of orphans who were left behind by this geno-cide. And yes, being in Immaculée's life in the small way that I am inspires me beyond anything that I can convey to you here in words.

— In 1999 I was invited to South Africa to lecture to some public audiences. While in Cape Town, I took the ferry over to Robben Island to visit the prison where Nelson Mandela had been incarcerated for so many years. (I actually visited at the time of the tenth-anniversary celebration of his release.)

Here was a man who spent more than 27 years of his life im-prisoned—he wasn't even allowed visitors because he was a vocal opponent of a system of apartheid, in which an entire race of peo-ple were declared by law to be inferior and unworthy of the same privileges as the remaining citizens of the country. And he worked all day in a limestone quarry, where the burning sunlight glared so against the white rock that his eyes became mere slits due to the squinting that he was forced to practice in order to survive. I spent 30 minutes in that quarry and my eyes stung all day—imagine what years of such exposure would wreak.

Mandela went deep within himself, and when he was finally released, he came out with forgiveness and reconciliation in his heart. His staying in-Spirit was the force behind the dismantling of apartheid and his ultimate election to the presidency of an emerging democracy of South Africa a few years later. As I medi-tated in the prison outside of this great man's cell, I felt the warm inner shower I described earlier in this chapter. Then I was handed an autographed copy of his book *Long Walk to Freedom,* which I treasure.

Nelson Mandela conveyed the spiritual energy of love, peace, kindness, and tolerance during all of his travails, and this spiritual energy provided a blueprint that changed the face of Africa—and the world—forever. Yes, he inspired me!

— Closer to home, I was inspired by Mrs. Olive Fletcher. In 1956 I was taking biology for the second time at Denby High School in

Detroit. I'd failed the class the previous year because of my own stubbornness: I'd refused to complete a leaf collection, which my then-15-year-old self perceived to be an absurd requirement.

At that time, my mother was divorcing my alcoholic step-father, and I was working in a local grocery store every evening during the week and all day on Saturday and Sunday. My instructor for this second foray into biology was Mrs. Fletcher, and she was the very first teacher I encountered who seemed to care about me personally. For example, she was there for me after school, called my home to see if I was okay during the tumultuousness (including frequent fights and other unpleasantness) taking place at the time, and allowed me to put my head down and sleep during study periods when I'd completed my assignments. She also encouraged me to tutor other students because she recognized something in me that I'd never heard a teacher say before: She told me that I was brilliant and had a mind that could take me wherever I wanted to go.

This incredible person even invited me to go bowling with her and her husband. I'd never imagined that teachers were actually human, let alone went bowling, before I met Mrs. Fletcher! She was also the first "authority figure" who welcomed my questioning and tolerated my sometimes disruptive behavior. By living from Spirit, she showed me that I was worth being loved by someone in a position of authority.

Thanks to Mrs. Fletcher's inspiration, I went from a failing grade the previous year to an A—I wanted to excel just for her because she had so much faith in me. Now, exactly a half century later, Mrs. Olive Fletcher still stands out as the one individual in all of my school years who turned the direction of my life from fighting the system to being able to choose to *fit in* without having to *give in*. Yes, she certainly inspired me!

— Switching gears a bit here, in 1971 Don McLean read a book on the life of the famous artist Vincent van Gogh and was so touched by the painter's fight for his sanity, along with his desire to be loved and understood, that he wrote a song about it.

Called "Vincent (Starry Starry Night)," it was written as he stared at van Gogh's classic painting *The Starry Night*—and every time I hear that song and recall how McLean was so inspired by the life of van Gogh, I'm inspired, too. I'm moved to tears, and I vow to be more understanding and compassionate toward those struggling with sanity as van Gogh did. (It's interesting to note that in the 1970s the Van Gogh Museum in Amsterdam played the song daily, and today a copy of the sheet music, together with a set of van Gogh's paintbrushes, is buried in a time capsule beneath the museum.)

I'm enormously inspired by people who act upon their own moments in-Spirit and create similar opportunities for countless souls as well. Don McLean moved me to read the same biography of van Gogh that he did and to include this example in this book. He inspired me!

I could write many more short descriptions of those who've provided me with life-altering inspiration, but I'd be remiss if I were to omit the one person among all those I've known who has been my greatest source of it.

Back in 1942, when I was two years old, my mother was left to take on the responsibility for raising my two brothers (ages three and five) and me alone. My father, of whom I have absolutely no recollection, literally walked out on his family and never once placed a phone call to see how we were doing. He paid no child support, since he spent a great deal of time in trouble with the law, including some jail time for being a thief. He simply walked away and never looked back.

After I was born, my mother brought me home to their tiny apartment on the east side of Detroit . . . and discovered that my father had left my 16-month-old brother, Dave, in the care of my 4-year-old brother, Jim, and had temporarily moved in with a woman in Ann Arbor, some 40 miles away.

Try to imagine the scene: *It's 1940. A depression has left almost everyone economically bankrupt. There are no government programs to aid the support of three children under the age of four. An alcoholic husband refuses to work, steals money from everyone, and regularly chooses the company of other women, leaving his wife to care for their three babies. An anemic infant needs medical assistance, which is largely unavailable to anyone living in poverty. . . .* Yet out of this seemingly hopeless scenario emerged a woman who had a dream that her life could and would get better.

After finally going through the divorce, my mother was totally on her own. She worked first as a candy girl at a five-and-dime store, and then as a secretary for the Chrysler Corporation—and her earnings came to approximately $17 per week. She was forced to place Dave and me in a series of foster homes supported by the Methodist church, while Jim moved in with her parents. Her nightmare was realized: Her family had been split up, and the thought of this being a permanent condition was too devastating for her to contemplate. But she held a vision for herself that she never ever abandoned: *Somehow, someday, I will unite my family and raise my boys under one roof.*

Unfortunately, times were challenging and the years passed. Mother visited Dave and me whenever possible. She didn't have an automobile or even a driver's license, and the distance to Mt. Clemens (where we resided) was approximately 17 miles. But it might as well have been 7,000 miles, since there was no transportation or money to pay for her to get there. But my mom was determined: She even married a man she didn't love as a way to unite her family.

In 1949, our family moved into a tiny, and I mean *tiny,* duplex on the east side of Detroit. Like our father, our new stepfather was also an alcoholic and an irresponsible provider. Drinking became his escape; and frequent, hostile interchanges were the norm. But Mother, who refused to see her boys separated again, continued to work, work, work.

Every morning she was up at 5 A.M., making breakfast and packing lunches for her three growing boys. She took three buses to work and three home every day, standing outside on those endless freezing winter mornings and returning home at 5:45 P.M. in order to prepare an evening meal. My brothers and I all had paper routes or were stock boys, but the hard work fell on the shoulders of this never-complaining, always-cheerful woman. Every weekend looked like this for my mother: washing endless loads of clothes and hanging them on the line to dry; making breakfast, lunch, and dinner; ironing down in the basement on Sundays. The work never ended . . . yet this woman was the most joyful, loving, beautiful soul to be around.

All my brothers' and my friends came to our house to hang out because of my mother. They loved her, and more than that, they loved being in our home because of the energy she brought to it. This woman lived from Spirit and offered all of us inspiration. Not one of us would ever have even considered talking back or being disrespectful in any way—she commanded our respect, but she never demanded it. And with all the responsibilities she had, Mother never left the house with her hair in curlers or her clothes in disarray—she took great pride in herself, and through her example, she taught my brothers and me to do the same.

While going through a second divorce from a now out-of-control alcoholic, she never abandoned her role as a mother to all of us. In later years when her own mother was quite sick, I watched in astonished admiration as she took on the sole responsibility for caring for her mom, despite the fact that she had four siblings. And then wonder of wonders, as my ex-stepfather reached a stage where his alcohol and smoking addictions were taking their final toll, I watched in amazement as she cared for this man who had largely mistreated her throughout their marriage. She went to his home, did his laundry, called for medical help, visited him in the hospital, and extended love where she had received only mistreatment and even abuse.

Today Mother approaches the age of 90 and still bowls twice a week, lives on her own, and never complains. To this day she won't leave home unless she's dressed to her high standards of appropriateness and her hair is beautifully coiffed. She respects herself, and this esteem has trickled down to me, her youngest son, and my two brothers as well. Now she has three boys who are all eligible for Social Security and Medicare, yet still she lives and breathes that loving Spirit.

In a wonderful book written by Michael Murphy called *What I Meant to Say,* he describes saying good-bye to his mother as he leaves her home after a Thanksgiving dinner. It's all small talk as he makes polite excuses for having to leave, which prompts the following tribute that I'm including here. I'd like to say these beautiful words to *my* mother:

What I meant to say was . . . How can I possibly say good-bye to the person who was the first to hold me, the first to feed me, and the first to make me feel loved?

From a distance I watch you move about, doing the mundane tasks that to everyone else seem so routine. But for me, the tasks you lovingly completed year after year built and reinforced the foundation, the structure that made my world a safe and comfortable place to grow.

All that I am and all that I have can be traced back to you. Whatever accomplishments I have made along the way would not have occurred without first believing in myself. And you, you were the person who always believed in me.

Now with a family of my own, I am amazed at the number of times I hear your words flow from my mouth. This ventriloquistic phenomenon was at first most irritating, but now warms me as I've come to understand that there is a part of you that will live on in me forever.

When time parts us, I pray that you will reach across from the other side to again touch my face and whisper into my ear.

For your warm and gentle presence in my life . . . for this, I will always be most thankful.

Yes, Mother, you inspire me!

Some Suggestions for Putting the Ideas in This Chapter to Work for You

— Make a deliberate decision to spend more time in the presence of those whom you're most closely aligned to in-Spirit. This means seeking out "higher-vibrational people" and avoiding those who reflect more ego-oriented behavior patterns. Keep in mind that higher spiritual energies nullify your lower tendencies, while also converting you to more in-Spirit frequencies. Use your own inner hunches to determine if you're in the right places with the right people: If you feel good in their presence, meaning that you feel inspired to be a better and more joyful person, then these are right for you. If, on the other hand, you feel more anxious, depressed, and uninspired, and you can't wait to get away because of conflict, then these are not going to be sources of inspiration for you.

— Read biographies of those people who reflect your ideas of high spiritual energy, be they historical or contemporary figures. Just by spending time reading about their lives, you'll feel a great sense of inspiration; moreover, their examples will serve to inspire you to emulate their lives and their greatness.

— Immerse yourself in movies, television shows, plays, and recordings tendered by individuals and organizations that reflect a rapport with Spirit. Simply listening to lectures by great spiritual teachers can increase your daily inspiration level.

Also, notice how you feel during explosion and chase scenes in movies that lead to an inevitable overexposure to violence, hatred, and killing. Check yourself in these moments: Do you feel closer to Spirit or further and further removed from It? Use your own intuition to remind yourself when it's time to change the channel or leave the movie theater. You have more control than you realize over who and what you allow into your mind and the minds of your loved ones, particularly your children. Exercise that control to stay connected to

Spirit. Invite into your heart only those energies that resonate with the desire to obey your ultimate calling to inspiration.

— Be clear about the distinctions between those you admire for their success in the physical world and those who are inspirational. The more you seek out and immerse yourself in ego-dominated energy fields, the more you'll feel disenchanted and lacking in joy. Use the tenets of Spirit to indicate what you desire to emulate, rather than using wealth or success as benchmarks.

Now while a successful person like Bill Gates may be a model for great fortune, it's important to realize that he and his wife have contributed more money and effort to the causes of literacy, healing, and peace than anyone else in the history of our planet. This stands in stark contrast to many of the "super rich" who use their money and status to further bolster their own ego. The Gateses represent high spiritual energy and serve as inspirational models for me, even though my financial picture doesn't even come close to theirs. I've learned from their actions, and I've found great inspiration from their in-Spirit philanthropy.

— Choose some of the most inspirational people in your life and tell them precisely why you've placed them in this category. As you relate your feelings and appreciation, you'll feel inspired merely by the simple act of acknowledgment. Every time I receive a letter or hear a personal testimony from someone who was inspired to pursue their own greatness because of my efforts, I'm touched and inspired myself. But I also know that the recognition and expression of that person's feelings means that they'll perform a similar service for others. And being in the service of others is really being more like God.

* * *

Ramakrishna, a great saint who lived in India and inspired millions of others from his God-realized perspective, once offered this observation: "[Saints] are like big steamships, which not only cross the ocean themselves but carry many passengers to the other shore." May you too be like those big steamships—but if you're not, then by all means allow yourself to be one of those lucky passengers.

Get on board by going on to the next chapter.

CHAPTER 11

BEING AN INSPIRATION FOR OTHERS

"We are all teachers, and what we teach is what we learn, and so we teach it over and over again until we learn . . ."

— FROM *A COURSE IN MIRACLES*

"The real purpose of teachers, books, and teachings is to lead us back to the kingdom of God within ourselves."

— JOEL GOLDSMITH

JUST AS WE'RE ALL STUDENTS THROUGHOUT LIFE, we're all teachers. In fact, we learn best by offering what we desire for ourselves to as many individuals as we can, as frequently as we can. And that's one reason I wrote this book: If I instruct enough people for a long enough period of time, I'll teach what *I* most want to learn, which is how to live in-Spirit. Following this line of thinking, it's imperative that we make a deliberate effort to increase our inspirational energy, as this will lead us to being both a spiritual learner and teacher simultaneously.

Spiritual teachers have raised the vibrational frequency of their daily life to a point where they're able to provide inspiration to others merely by their presence, and this is the standard to which we need to aspire. It isn't necessarily a scholarly undertaking—there are no lesson plans or report cards for the kind of teaching I'm writing about in these pages. Rather, I'm talking about the things we can do each and every day to inspire our fellow humans . . . which is what this chapter is all about.

Kindness Inspires Others

Recently three of my kids and I were seated at the food court of a mall here on Maui. As we were talking and enjoying our meals, a young boy stumbled, and the tray full of hamburgers and French fries he'd just purchased from McDonald's went flying all over the floor. His parents immediately came to his rescue, and the manager of the restaurant good-naturedly replaced all of the food at no cost. The boy was embarrassed, but it all worked out fine . . . except that people were having to dodge what he'd dropped as they lined up for their purchases.

Neither the boy's family nor the people working at the restaurant took any initiative to clean up this mess, which was actually a hazard to the crowd at the food court. I watched for a few moments, and then I took an empty tray and proceeded to pick up all of the food and dispose of it in the trash container. I returned to my seat, saying nothing about the incident.

About ten minutes later, a woman who'd observed this scene without my noticing came over to our table. To my teenagers she said, "You girls have just been given a lesson by your father—he has shown you by his actions what it means to be a caring, helpful citizen. No one else in this entire place thought of doing anything about that mess on the floor, but he did. He inspired me, and I hope that you were inspired by his actions, too." She left, and my girls sort of smiled knowingly, since this is rather a normal thing for them to see.

The point of this story is to illustrate that one simple act of kindness and service that's in alignment with our Source will do more to inspire others than lectures on the virtues of being a thoughtful citizen ever could. All I wanted to do was eliminate the potential peril of greasy burgers and fries on the floor—I wasn't trying to inspire anyone—and that's the crux of this chapter.

When we elevate our consciousness above the level of ego, which says, "I didn't spill that food, so it's not my job to clean it up!" to the level that asks, "How may I serve?" we become an inadvertent source of inspiration to anyone who's in the energy field of our spiritually based actions.

We can also be on the lookout for opportunities to be a source of inspiration. For example, when I board an airplane, I tend to look for the chance to extend some sort of service to "strangers." (I put the word in quotes to emphasize that there aren't actually any strangers anywhere in the Universe.) Helping vertically challenged passengers place their carry-on luggage in the overhead compartment is perfect because others noticing this act of kindness may be inspired, while, at the same time, I'm heeding my own calling to be both inspired and inspiring.

I know that someone who needs my assistance is really a Divine emissary who's right there in front of me, offering an opportunity for me to be in-Spirit. For instance, not long ago I flew from Maui to Los Angeles and then boarded an all-night flight to New York. On the way to L.A., I'd watched the fabulous movie *Chicago;* once on the plane to New York, I noticed one of the stars of that film, Renée Zellweger, getting on. Vertically challenged with heavy luggage, she certainly met all of my criteria for being both a source of inspiration and becoming inspired. I helped her with her baggage and then gave her a copy of my book *10 Secrets for Success and Inner Peace.*

Many people on the plane approached her, including the flight attendants, and I watched and felt inspired by the kindness, patience, and personal concern Renée showed toward everyone she talked to. As we left the plane, she handed me a note that I've reproduced on the next page, exactly as she wrote it, to illustrate how everyday acts of kindness serve as memorable moments of inspiration. Sharing it here with you is a way to express my gratitude for her thoughtfulness—what a bonus!

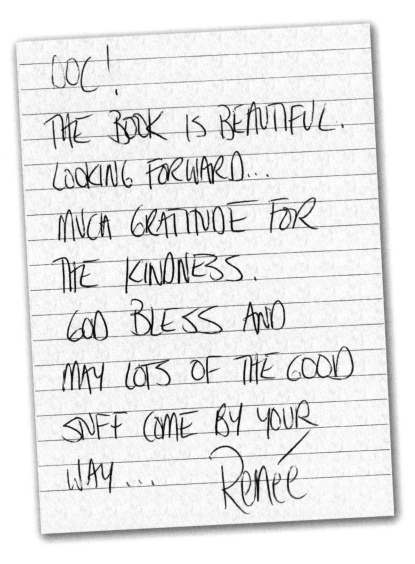

> OOC!
>
> THE BOOK IS BEAUTIFUL.
> LOOKING FORWARD...
> MUCH GRATITUDE FOR
> THE KINDNESS.
> GOD BLESS AND
> MAY LOTS OF THE GOOD
> STUFF COME BY YOUR
> WAY...   Renée

To this day, whenever I see Renée in a movie or an interview, I recall the extraordinary, gentle kindness that she displayed toward everyone who approached her, and it inspires me. My moment or two of extending service to her was a gift to *me,* not because she's a celebrity, but because of that dual reward of being in-Spirit.

Gratitude Inspires Others

Without exception, I begin every day of my life with an expression of gratitude. As I look in the mirror to begin my daily ritual of shaving, I say, "Thank you, God, for life, for my body, for my family and loved ones, for this day, and for the opportunity to be of service. Thank you, thank you, thank you!"

If we practice gratitude as opposed to maintaining an attitude of entitlement, we'll automatically extend inspiration wherever we go. Being grateful helps remove the influence of our ego, which is certain that we're better than everyone else. An attitude of gratitude allows us to adopt what's called "radical humility," a trait that's very persuasive in helping others feel inspired.

Most of the people I've met or observed who are at the top levels in their chosen fields have these attitudes of gratitude and radical humility. After all, when so many high achievers reach for their statuette or championship trophy, they say, "First I'd like to thank God." It's almost as if they can't help themselves—they're so grateful for their accolade, but even more than that, they know that there's a Force in the Universe way bigger than they are that allows them to act, sing, write, compete, or design. And if *we* adopt this kind of an attitude, we'll inspire others. It's that simple.

Pomposity, on the other hand, will never inspire anyone. When we encounter someone who brags and uses the pronoun *I* excessively, we'll find that we want to get away from them as quickly as possible. Vanity, conceit, and boasting are all signs that a person has **e**dged **G**od **o**ut of the picture.

Gratitude and humility, on the other hand, send signals to all who meet and greet us that we're all connected to something larger than life itself. This reminds me of the wisdom I discovered many years ago reading the Kena Upanishad: "At whose bequest does the mind think? Who bids the body live? Who makes the tongue speak? Who is the effulgent Being that directs eye to form and color, and the ear to sound?" When we know the answer to these questions, we not only become inspiring beings to others, we also gain immortality.

Generosity Inspires Others

It doesn't matter if we call It God, Krishna, Atman, Allah, the Universal Mind, Ra, Yahweh, or even Anna or Fred—I think we'd all agree that the All-Creating Source of Everything is the most generous Being there is. Along with life itself, It offers us unending abundance in the form of air, water, lungs, heart, kidneys, liver, and all we need to sustain life. On just this one tiny planet hurtling through space, Whatever Name We Want to Call It provides the ability to feed all of us and dispose of all of our waste, which then gets used to fertilize new life—and then repeats the process over and over again. . . . And remember, this is only one planet in an endless Universe of heavenly bodies. Talk about benevolence!

Generosity is obviously one of the ways to be more God-like. I know that I'm inspired when I see evidence of it on the part of others. Very often it's manifested during or following times of crisis, almost as if God gets our attention and reminds us to be more like Him when we face devastating circumstances. A tsunami diverts our aircraft carriers away from killing each other and into a zone where food and shelter are offered; an earthquake motivates us to risk our own lives to save strangers who days before were called enemies; and hurricanes bring out the best in us. Such so-called disasters lead us to the inherent God-like generosity that's latent within all of us. However, we don't need a crisis to remind ourselves to give—we only need to be in-Spirit to be reminded of the joy of donating our energy, time, and possessions to others.

For example, my brother Jim and my sister-in-law Marilyn are inspiring because of the time they give to our mother. Days spent going to movies and playing *Scrabble* are more than just entertaining activities—they're inspiration in action because Jim and Marilyn are giving their time to lovingly be with a person who lives alone. While I've been blessed to be able to give to Mother financially, they've been blessed to give of their time.

Generous actions are always inspirational if we just spend a few seconds to notice and appreciate them. The message is that *we must give whatever it is we have that will benefit others.* It's how our Creator conducts Itself—always giving and providing. When we emulate our Creator by giving, we become sources of inspiration to others.

When Oprah Winfrey visited Africa and vowed to give all that she could, including money and time, to help eradicate the poverty and disease of that continent, she inspired me and millions of others. When she said, "Now I know why I have been given so much. Now I know why," I also began saying to myself, "Now I know why *I've* had so many financial blessings. I feel so grateful for all that has come my way that giving back seems to be the only avenue available."

I was inspired by the generosity of a woman I've known for 30 years, who also came from an impoverished background, to set up a scholarship fund at my alma mater, Wayne State University. Oprah's philanthropy inspired me, and I hope that I in turn will inspire young people to do the same with their lives. Think of the incredible good that would come if people who read this book also became inspired to give. Of course we don't have to be wealthy to give, but we might need to remember this: *If we're not generous when it's difficult, we won't be generous when it's easy.*

Listening Inspires Others

As ironic as it may sound, we're far more inspiring to others when we're willing to listen than when we're giving them advice. That's because conveying to others that we value what they have to say is a way of demonstrating that we care. It's a way of being inspiring, a way of listening like God. People who find it difficult to listen to another person without bringing the conversation back to themselves are convinced by their ego of their self-importance. And as you're well aware by now, that ego is an illusion that's convinced us to pay attention to a false self.

There's no higher compliment than to be told we're a good listener. Everyone loves a good listener largely because it makes them feel loved, cared for, and worthy of being heard. When we leave any encounter where we feel we've been heard, even if we know the listener strongly disagreed with us, we're still inspired. Why? Because for a few moments the listener has emulated what it feels like when we pray. In deep prayer, we're not looking for the resolution of conflict or answers falling from the sky; we just want to feel as if we're in contact with someone who cares enough to hear us out.

This brings to mind something Mohandas Gandhi, one of the truly inspirational beings of our time, once said: "Silence of the sewn up lips is no silence. One may achieve the same result by chopping off one's tongue, but that too would not be silence. He is truly silent who, having the capacity to speak, utters no idle word . . ."

In addition, these words from Ralph Waldo Emerson have always reminded me to be a listener: "I like the silent church, before the service begins, better than the preaching." It's a good idea to keep this in mind if we wish to be a source of inspiration.

Being at Peace Inspires Others

Lecturing or demanding that others live peacefully is one of the least effective ways to inspire them; however, when we simply demonstrate that we're living peacefully, we offer other people a large dose of inspiration by our mere presence.

During my first encounter with Swami Satchidananda, for instance, he emitted such an aura of peacefulness that I felt inspired by merely standing next to him. It would have been impossible for me to feel anything other than peace in his midst. That day I purchased his wonderful book, *Beyond Words,* and on page 21 was given an inkling as to why I felt so inspired merely by being in his company: "If anybody asks me, 'What is your philosophy of God?' I say, 'Peace is my God.' If they ask, 'Where is He?' I reply, 'He is in me and He is everywhere. He is all peaceful; He is all serenity. He is to be felt and experienced within oneself.'"

Being at peace with ourselves is a way of going through life eschewing conflict and confrontation. When we're in a state of tranquility, we actually send out a vibration of energy that impacts all living creatures, including plants, animals, and all people (even babies). And, of course, the reverse applies as well: Belligerent individuals who live in turmoil and revel in hostile encounters send out nonverbal energy that adversely impacts those around them. The immediate impulse is to remove ourselves from these low-energy, nonpeaceful people because sticking around means tension and a lowering of our energy. Moreover, we become a counterforce to what we're experiencing, meaning that we become angry at their anger and arrogant toward their arrogance.

Practicing a peaceful approach to our life on Earth is a way of returning to where we came from. At the same time, it's a powerful source of inspiration to all living creatures.

Living Passionately Inspires Others

Did you know that the word *enthusiasm* originated from the Greek language, signifying "the God within us"? By definition, then, living our passion is the way to convey to others how to be in-Spirit. Being excited about life is infectious—it rubs off on others and is wonderfully inspiring. I'm reminded of a recent whale-watching trip I took, where I observed a young woman I know named Beth as she spoke to a group of people about humpback whales. Her enthusiasm was palpable to the entire group aboard the boat, and the more passion she displayed, the more she seemed to inspire her audience. I've been aboard other boats and seen the impact of guides who merely go through the motions: People in this low-energy environment don't leave the experience feeling inspired.

Beth, on the other hand, feels a passion that she conveys to others every single day during the whale-mating season. Every day! You see, she studied marine biology in college and has always been fascinated by humpback whales and their amazing ability to travel between Alaska and Hawaii, to go six months without eating, to give birth in warm waters, and then navigate to cold waters on the return. For Beth, these whales are a part of God's mysterious, miraculous creation. She's living her passion, and she inspires others by her enthusiastic way of being. In fact, everyone in this vicinity knows that expeditions with Beth are almost a guarantee that you'll not only get to see the whales, but that they'll dance and breach and even swim under the boat for you. It's as if the whales themselves are inspired by Beth's excitement!

When we're enthusiastically living our passion, whatever it may be, we transmit spiritual signals to those around us that we're in-Spirit, loving who we are, what we came here to be, and whoever comes into our field of vision.

Truth Inspires Others

Finally, and perhaps most urgently, we need to live and breathe truth because nothing inspires other people more than being in its energy field. Years ago I wrote an article called "Who Do You Trust?" in which I explained that the trust issue rests on who we seek out when we want truth. Are we drawn to those who'll tell us what we want to hear or those who are unafraid to be honest with us, even if it might be unpleasant or difficult for us to hear? The answer is obvious: We prefer to hear the truth.

Honesty is a necessity if we're ever to live in harmony with Spirit and become a source of inspiration for others as well. When we shade the truth, a part of our brain registers this incongruity— it shows up as a disconnect from God, and we're out of balance. Our body reacts by becoming weaker in the face of any falsehood, including our attachment to the false self known as ego. As we practice living and speaking from our truth without being hurtful or arrogant in any way, we reconnect with the energy we emanated from in the first place.

In kinesiology there's a procedure called muscle testing, where the body is used as a veritable lie detector. In other words, if a person isn't telling the truth, their muscles are weaker than when they're answering honestly. They can't hold their arm up or their fingers together against applied pressure when they're thinking a falsehood; yet when they shift to a truthful thought, with the same pressure applied, they're able to withstand the same force. Try it, and you'll be amazed. It turns out that experimenters have discovered that the body, an instrument of God's creation, is stronger when it's directed by honesty. Since Spirit creates only out of truth, a thought of truth is in harmony with God's truth. (The entire procedural blueprint, along with instructions on how to use the body as a "lie detector," is readily explained in *Power vs. Force,* written by David Hawkins and published by Hay House.)

So let's remember truth as a means for inspiring each other. We must be unafraid to live and speak our truth—think how inspiring we'd all be for each other if honesty was a prominent feature of our interactions. By demonstrating 100 percent commitment to truth, with no exceptions, we send out a signal that we're in accord with our Source, and we'll do more to inspire others to live and breathe from their own truth than a thousand readings of the Ten Commandments or any other written document.

Truth and God are one. We don't have to preach it, only *live it*—by doing so, we'll radiate it to everyone we come into contact with. As an ancient Hindu saying reminds us, "The name of God is truth."

Some Suggestions for Putting the Ideas in This Chapter to Work for You

— Work on becoming more peaceful, and start noticing how you're perceived by others. Practice daily meditation to become more peaceful, and then watch as others who previously engaged you in confrontation are less inclined in that direction. Decide for yourself that you're an emissary of peace and that that's precisely the energy you're going to radiate wherever you go. By lifting your thoughts upward so that they resonate with the peace that divines your origination, you'll automatically become a person who inspires others to do the same, without having to adopt any new strategies and with an absence of "effort" on your part.

— Actively work at reducing your inclinations to interrupt others with an *I* reference in conversations. Just "stifle yourself," as Archie Bunker used to say. Make a concerted effort to be silent when you're about to interrupt. See the words *stifle yourself* flash on your inner screen, and remind yourself at that moment that you inspire by listening and encouraging, not by self-reference or sermonizing.

— Before speaking, consult your inner "truth barometer" and resist the temptation to tell people what they want to hear if that feels untrue to you. People do respect those who are willing to speak their truth, and even more, to *live* the truth they feel. When I write an article, for instance, I know precisely who to show it to for comments if I want a guaranteed set of compliments to come my way—but I also know who's unafraid to come from their truth, and this is where I seek feedback. Not that someone else's truth will automatically match up with mine, but at least I'm hearing from a person who lives and speaks from their own inner fidelity. This kind of person inspires me by being aligned with our place of origin, which is, of course, pure honesty. You can be this inspiring kind of a person by abandoning your need for approval and replacing it with authenticity and integrity.

— Let everyone you meet know that there's one thing about you that isn't up for discussion: You are going to live your passion, and there's absolutely no room for compromise on this point. Carry yourself proudly and show your enthusiasm in all of your waking hours. Be passionate about all of your activities, and keep reminding yourself that you will never elect apathy or ennui. Never! By refusing to concede this point, you'll become a model for others to live out *their* lives in-Spirit.

When I speak to audiences, I'm always aware that by my being in-Spirit and conveying this vibration to them, I'm offering everyone there an opportunity to do the same for themselves. When beginning speakers ask me for advice on how to become an in-demand lecturer, my answer is always the same: "Talk from your heart authentically and be enthusiastic." Passionate, truthful communication is always inspiring.

— Practice being generous as often as you can. Promise yourself to extend some kind of unexpected generosity to someone, preferably a stranger, every single day for two weeks. This will not only help you develop a habit of giving, but you'll also discover how wonderfully inspiring your generous nature feels. The more you practice being charitable, the more you'll impact others in an inspiring way. By letting others know that you're willing to give of your time as well as your possessions, you'll serve as an inspirational model. Who isn't inspired by those who're willing to share their time, money, and possessions? We name cities (San Francisco) for such people and we nominate them (Mother Teresa) for sainthood . . . you too can inspire by being a benevolent soul.

Also practice tithing (giving 10 percent of what you earn in a given period to support teaching that provides you with spiritual uplift) and see if it doesn't return to you tenfold. This has worked for me my entire life, and continues as I practice my natural instinct to be generous.

❋ ❋ ❋

In an exceptionally inspiring book titled *Season of Life*, Jeffrey Marx, a Pulitzer Prize–winning writer, chronicles a high school football team in which a former player with the Baltimore Colts named Joe Ehrmann is on the coaching staff. His coaching philosophy is to "help boys become men within the context of sports"— that is, without threats, screaming, or violence.

"I expect greatness out of you," the team's head coach tells his players, "and the way we measure greatness is the impact you make on other people's lives." As the ten coaches and assistant coaches huddle with the team on game day, one of them asks, "What is our job?" "To love us!" the team yells back in unison. "And what is *your* job?" the coach asks. "To love each other," the team responds. This is the philosophy that these boys were exposed to every day—at practice, on the field, and during and after the games—and so it goes for all of us who wish to inspire others. We must love all others and teach them to love each other. After all, in the Talmud we're told that "God said: you must teach, as I taught, without a fee . . ."

Inspiring others and becoming inspired ourselves involves being more like our Creator, since true teaching is about leading others back to the Spirit that's within everyone.

CHAPTER 12

TRANSCENDING COMMONPLACE, UNINSPIRING ENERGY

"For all our insight, obstinate habits do not disappear until replaced by other habits . . . No amount of confession and no amount of explaining can make the crooked plant grow straight; it must be trained upon the trellis by the gardener's art . . ."

— CARL JUNG

"Habit rules the unreflecting herd."

— WILLIAM WORDSWORTH

THANKS TO THE WORLD WE LIVE IN, we've developed many habits that are the direct result of living almost exclusively "in-ego" rather than in-Spirit. This chapter will stress how to gain awareness of these ego habits, how to immediately protect ourselves from these onslaughts, and how to develop alternate strategies to ensure that we remain connected to Spirit—even in the face of a blitzkrieg that's designed to take us away from living an inspired life.

I'm not suggesting that there's a conspiracy to keep us from living in-Spirit. My contention is simply that when a majority of society members are raised and persuaded to believe in the illusion of ego, then that society will develop and evolve firmly committed to that false self. It would then be natural for such a society to put forth messages designed to promote the idea of the importance of ego and all of its inherent ideas—and we're fully immersed in just such a society.

I once heard Swami Satchidananda lecture about this subject of the collective ego and its unceasing impact on all of us. He looked at the two words *heart* and *head,* the symbols for Spirit and ego, respectively, and confirmed that we're in-Spirit when we act from our heart. Swami also observed that the word *heart* contains two words, *he* and *art,* and that leads to the thought that *he and his art* make up the heart.

The word *head,* on the other hand, also contains two words—*he* and *ad*—which leads to the thought that *he and his ad make up the head.* Swami reminded us that the head is an advertisement—that is, it's the ego looking for recognition. He then asked a question I've never forgotten: "Why is it that lovers call each other sweet-*heart* and not sweet*head?*" And he reminded us not to despise the head or symbolically cut it off, but rather to let our heart (that is, our feelings) lead, and the head will then follow, rather than the other way around. To that end, this chapter provides three steps to help us transcend the ego's uninspiring energy. They are: *becoming aware, cultivating a defense,* and *developing our own alternatives.*

Ego's Warriors

Let's first take a look at some of the "habits that rule the herd," in the words of William Wordsworth. Following are several omnipresent, lacking-in-inspiration entities that join up with ego to bombard us daily, and that we need to become aware of.

The Media

A century or so ago, long before the media became such an active force in our lives, the news was almost exclusively received from one's village. Bad news was rare, and tended to only involve accidents or natural disasters, such as fire, flood, drought, or the occasional crime perpetrated by someone in the community. For the most part, one's daily life was consumed by work and family interaction—any kind of news was essentially information about the village and was primarily communicated by word of mouth.

Today, however, it's a very different picture. We've created a society that sends out specially trained people to scour the globe for depressing bulletins that are delivered to us wherever we are. The news is now available at home, at work, in our car, at the gym, on airplanes, standing in line at the bank, in the hospital, and on portable devices wherever we go. We're now able to directly tune in to the reports of those organizations who search for information designed to make us feel bad—that is, removed from Spirit, which is all about feeling good (God).

An explosion on the other side of the planet? We get a continual video loop. A suicide bomber in the Middle East kills 75 people? We get to see it all in grisly detail. A man stabs his wife and children anywhere in the country, and we get to hear about it on our local 11 o'clock news—thanks to an eyewitness reporter who's interviewing every neighbor willing to go on camera. . . .

We're constantly subjected to this army of bad-news collectors who gather and disseminate low-vibrational energy for our consumption. Keeping in mind that being inspired is about feeling good and returning to our Source of love, it's imperative to become aware of what we're allowing into our consciousness. These bad-news assemblers are on a mission to convince us of the inherent evil in the world—they can't possibly believe that we live in a friendly Universe, and they seem determined to convince us that their illusion is truth.

As we become aware that we're paying attention to uninspiring reports that are directed at us in the guise of keeping us informed, we can begin to take the necessary steps to return to Spirit. First, we must be aware that this "news" is more accurately a steady dose of low energy that's addictive. When we watch or listen to such messages, we can simply check in with our heart self and ask, "Is this a match to how I want to feel? If I continue to stay connected to these energies, will I feel good (God) or bad?"

Note that there are hundreds of cable news channels that need to fill 24 hours a day of broadcasting. Consequently, the analysts of these shows must dissect every crime, horrible accident, and bit of conflict they can find, and they must also maintain a confrontational attitude with whomever they're talking—or more likely, arguing—with. Being a match to the originating Spirit of Well-Being and Peace is close to impossible in such situations.

I'm not suggesting that we stay uninformed or in a state of blissful ignorance; rather, I'm saying that awareness is the key to staying in-Spirit when we're force-fed a steady diet of low-energy news. We simply need to become aware of what we've decided to allow into our space when we're online, watching television, or reading a newspaper. By catching ourselves when we're getting worked up, we can then begin to defend against these assaults on our spirituality. And we can start by asking ourselves this question: "Do I feel good right now?"

The defense against a media blitz of uninspiring energies is to remind ourselves that we want to feel good, in the sense that *good* and *God* are synonymous. We can't feel bad enough to change any of the bad news we're exposed to, nor can we eliminate hatred in the world by feeling hateful—we can't do anything positive or loving by joining those who've elected to live in these energies, or even those who broadcast it to us nonstop. However, by feeling good (God), we have an opportunity to be a small force that can transcend and convert lower energies into spiritual ones.

Our alternative to feeling down when we're exposed to a media offense of bad news is to instantly remind ourselves that we refuse to be a vibrational match to anything uninspiring. So, armed with this defense, we can become informed as well as inspired—and we'll ultimately reach a point where we remember that we're not accepting uninspiring energy any longer. Lo and behold, by being more like God (rather than more like ego), we actually will make a dent in all of the negativity that's delivered to us via the various faces of the media. By successfully opting for alternatives to the bad news and the political quarreling, we'll choose to remain in-Spirit and feel good (God), regardless of how many others wish to live as if they're in a pitched battle where conflict and agitation rule.

The World of Advertising

Everywhere we turn, we're a target of someone wanting to sell us something. There are advertisements on buses, in the backseat of cabs, at the movies, on telephone poles, on our cell phones, after every click of our computers, on the radio and television for more than a third of the airtime, in more than 50 percent of magazine pages (in most cases, anyway), while we're on hold on the telephone, and even in restrooms! It's difficult to escape this assault on our senses and our spirit as well. Behind this huge blitz that's aimed at us during every waking moment of our lives is the idea that we need to purchase something in order to be "fixed" or "complete." Madison Avenue just keeps telling us that we'll overcome our deficiencies and be happier and more fulfilled if we simply buy whatever it is they're selling! The essential message behind this juggernaut is that we need *more* in order to be happy. Coincidentally, the mantra of the ego is just that: *more, more, more.*

Ego insists on believing that we don't have enough, others have more, there's newer and better stuff, we won't be liked unless we purchase that thing, we lack status, and some designer label will make life better. This is the exact opposite of what Spirit gently whispers, which is: "You are complete already, a product of universal abundance, so relax and enjoy life . . . what you desire will show up with less effort and no anxiety."

The first step in transcending the uninspiring messages that besiege us to buy more is to *become aware of what's going on and realize that we don't really need anything else in order to be happy.* After all, there's no way to happiness—happiness *is* the way. We may need to say this to ourselves over and over until it sinks in: "Nothing can make me happy. Happiness and inspiration are what I bring to life, not what I purchase." This awareness diminishes the annoyance of all those commercial messages, and at the same time allows us to enjoy the creativity of the advertising industry, because we've detached from the ego messages and connected to Spirit. Knowing that we don't need any more things in order to have a more complete life means that we can either ignore the pressure to buy or enjoy it. With awareness and a reconnection to Spirit comes the realization that ads aren't directed at our authentic self—and when we choose to stay in-Spirit, this awareness becomes its own defense.

What I'm suggesting is that we can be free from the push to convince us that we need more, while still being able to enjoy the material aspects of the world. In other words, we know that we don't *need* more, and at the same time, we're free to live happily and enjoy our world the way it is. I want this distinction to be clear because it's fun enjoying a new automobile, well-made clothes, dinner in a nice restaurant, an expensive piece of jewelry, or anything else that might be advertised (including this book). What we want to avoid is the inner belief that somehow our true essence is lacking if we don't get the things we're being encouraged to buy. We must also guard against allowing this "stuff" to define our worthiness, which is what advertisers are frequently attempting to convey.

When I allowed my awareness to purchase only what I desired, thus maintaining my sense of true inspiration, I found myself less and less attached to *stuff*. You see, the more I have, the more it becomes almost burdensome to store it, insure it, dust it, decide if it's tax deductible, and ultimately dispose of it. These days I'm almost amused by the advertising I'm subjected to, and when it appears, I press my "spiritual mute button" and feel even happier that I'm immune to the invitations of advertisers to add their brand of status to my life.

Another thing I've noticed that's a considerable impediment to living a life in-Spirit is the content of ads. They're designed to convince us that we're inherently powerless in the face of illness and stress when it shows up in our body. To begin with, our body is the most amazing pharmacy ever created, and it's perfectly capable of manufacturing and distributing whatever healing materials we need. Our body originated from a stream of pure well-being, so when we feel depressed, anxious, fearful, or whatever, our brain can create whatever prescription it needs.

I'm not disparaging the magnificent strides that modern medicine has made in helping us all to live healthier, more fulfilling lives. However, I *am* alarmed by the recent phenomenon of large pharmaceutical companies in bed with the medical profession, inundating our airwaves with messages designed to get us to ask our doctor to prescribe a pill for every real or imagined malady. Almost 50 percent of prime-time television shows are sponsored by drug companies, promoting items that can only be prescribed by a licensed physician. We're being sold the idea that we need a variety of pills to feel better, walk better, breathe better, sleep better, play better, and even make love better! Also appearing as three- and four-page announcements in national magazines, these ads are contrived to put our health and happiness in the profit-motivated hands of drug companies and physicians—at the expense of our living an inspired life. It's a veritable invasion of our spirit.

We're in a body that has a natural tendency toward health and can overcome almost anything if we allow it to perform its own magic, so we must be cautious about the motivations of companies that want us to become hooked on medicine that can conveniently be prescribed for a lifetime. We probably don't need to rely on something manufactured in a laboratory and sold by a huge pharmaceutical conglomerate whose primary objective is skyrocketing profits through advertising; rather, by practicing awareness, we can be in-Spirit and rely on our body's own pharmacy and doctor in one miraculous spiritual package.

Entertainment

As we progress toward a more inspired life, we'll begin to notice that the activities we've called "entertainment" have actually been leading us away from being in-Spirit. Since everything that we allow into our life represents an energy that impacts us both physically and spiritually, it's imperative to raise our awareness level and defend against the habits that deter us from being in-Spirit.

Reflect on Wordsworth's observation at the opening of this chapter: "Habit rules the unreflecting herd." We certainly don't want to be either unreflecting or part of a herd because as we know, when we follow the herd, we end up stepping in herd poop! Thus, we need to sharpen our awareness of the habits we've developed that camouflage uninspiring activities—it's all too common in our society to believe that nonspiritual energies are an important part of our entertainment package.

It's vital that we're conscious of the following "big four," which are really low-level energies masquerading as entertainment and are obstacles to anyone's ultimate calling to inspiration.

1. Violence. On average, children in America see 12,000 simulated murders in their own home on commercial and cable television before their 14th birthday; and virtually all movies made to appeal to a younger audience have grim killings, explosions, and chase scenes built into the story line, which seems to consist of "guns, guns, guns, and kill, kill, kill—the more gruesomely, the better."

These decidedly uninspiring messages continually bombard all of us when we're supposedly experiencing uplifting entertainment, but we can do something about it. If enough of us decide that this is not going to be on our daily menu, then the manufacturers of this kind of recreational material would bring it to a halt. For example, if more of us were aware of the content of the video games that our kids play—many of which simulate rape, torture, and even murder—we wouldn't permit them in our homes.

In addition, sporting events that are supposed to be entertaining to spectators are increasingly being tainted by escalating levels of violence. It's become commonplace for athletes to take steroids to make them bigger and more ferocious, and fans applauding hotheaded cheap shots and encouraging melees to break out is considered entertaining. Even the music being written and performed today often contains messages of violence and profanity. And I could go on and on with an inventory of the violence and bloodthirstiness that's prevalent in the entertainment industry (as you practice being more aware, I'm sure you'll add examples to this list, too).

Yet there are alternatives available to us. First on this list is screening our entertainment options for violence and making a commitment to choose only those pastimes that are free of any energy that doesn't match our desire to be in-Spirit. Our Creator creates out of love, kindness, and peace, so if we clear opposite energies out of our life, we'll almost immediately feel inspiration returning to our life.

What follows is one of the most poignantly inspiring letters I've ever read, written by my dear friend Ram Dass to the parents of a young girl who'd been brutally murdered. Even in such horrific circumstances, Ram Dass was able to provide inspiration. I reproduce this moving letter with Ram Dass's permission in order to help you see how it is possible to transcend violence with inspiring spiritual energy.

> *Dear Steve and Anita,*
>
> *Rachel finished her work on Earth and left the stage in a manner that leaves those of us left behind with a cry of agony in our hearts, as the fragile thread of our faith is dealt with so violently. Is anyone strong enough to stay conscious through such teaching as you are receiving? Probably very few. And even they would only have a whisper of equanimity and peace amidst the screaming trumpets of their rage, grief, horror, and desolation.*
>
> *I can't assuage your pain with any words, nor should I, for your pain is Rachel's legacy to you. Not that she or I would inflict such pain by choice, but there it is. And it must burn its purifying way to completion. For something in you dies when you bear the unbearable, and it is only in that dark night of the soul that you are prepared to see as God sees, and to love as God loves.*
>
> *Now is the time to let your grief find expression—no false strength. Now is the time to sit quietly and speak to Rachel, thank her for being with you these few years, and encourage her to go on with whatever her work is, knowing that you will grow in compassion and wisdom from this experience. In my heart, I know that you and she will meet again and again, and recognize the many ways in which you have known each other.*

*And when you meet you will know, in a flash, what now it is
not given to you to know: why this had to be the way it was.*

*Our rational minds can never understand what has hap-
pened, but our hearts—if we keep them open to God—will
find their own intuitive way. Rachel came through you to do
her work on Earth, which includes her manner of death. Now
her soul is free, and the love that you can share with her is
invulnerable to the winds of changing time and space. In that
deep love, include me.*

In love,

Ram Dass

2. Hatred. Much of our entertainment dollar is spent watching malice, hatred, and hostility in some form. Now in my opinion,
there's far too much animosity in our world, so I have no desire
to sit through a movie or listen to a song that repeatedly describes
how one group hates another. Martin Luther King, Jr., one of my
personal heroes, said that the only way to convert a perceived
enemy into a friend is by love. Since we know that hatred itself
breeds more of the same, then being exposed to it—even when
it's dressed up as entertainment—is something to be cognizant of
when we choose a film, television show, sporting event, play, or
book. *Any* hateful message is nonspiritual energy that we're expos-
ing ourselves to . . . and the more we consciously allow, the more
we'll be inclined to attract in our life.

The moral of all of this is that entertainment can be uplifting
and edifying, or it can be demoralizing and debasing. So where
do we want our energy to flow—and, even more important, what
kind of energy do we want our children to experience? We must
be on guard against any entertainment that uses excessive profanity and seems to support hatred and disrespect in its narrative.

I love this story that the Dalai Lama told in a documentary
titled *The Yogis of Tibet*. It seems that one of the most enlightened Tibetan yogis who witnessed the carnage and decimation
of the entire Tibetan culture by the Chinese, beginning with the
Communist Revolution of Mao Tse-tung in 1949, related a story

in which he stated several times, "I was in great danger." This was surprising, since these yogis cared very little about their own safety. When the enlightened yogi was asked about his perceived danger, he responded, "Yes, yes, I *was* in grave danger. That is, I was in danger of losing my compassion for the Chinese."

This is not only a beautiful story, but it also helps us remember to be careful about accepting hatred as normal in our entertainment activities, for they can put us in the same kind of danger that the enlightened yogi recognized. And even more personally significant, enjoying hatred as entertainment can keep us from reconnecting to inspiration.

3. Fear. A quick review of today's morning paper reveals that a killer is on the loose, there are new terrorist threats to the U.S. and more terrorist threats in Spain, global warming is melting the polar ice caps, deaths at rail crossings have increased 11 percent in one year, gasoline prices are increasing and automobile sales are declining, OPEC's cutting off the oil supply, frequent-flier miles probably won't be redeemable because the airlines have nine trillion miles they owe us, the expectation of a heavy-duty forest-fire season is high, hurricane devastation will increase in the next ten years . . . and I'm only on page three!

Every day we're inundated with urgent messages to live in fear by our news-gathering agencies, our movies, our television programming, and even our government. Try buying anything to consume without having to remove layer after layer of protective seals to keep out all of the monsters who are trying to poison our foods. As a child I recall slurping from a garden hose—today we fear the toxins in our drinking water. I recall riding my bike all day in my Levi's and a T-shirt—today we fear brain injuries and require helmets and protective gear just to ride a bicycle. I recall talking to strangers and trusting their good intentions—today everyone is a potential predator. I recall being home when the streetlights came on and never having to call home to reassure my mother that I was safe—today every child needs a cell phone and lives in fear of being abducted.

We've become a fear-based society, and this dread has crept into all facets of our lives, including our entertainment. We sit in movie theaters biting our fingernails as we watch the machinations of a serial killer or see someone being decapitated by a chain saw. We're told a thousand times a day to live in fear and worry about one kind of disaster or another: Someone is going to rob us or set our house on fire, a natural disaster is on its way, and the television beseeches us to watch *Fear Factor*. I could go on and on here, but I'm sure you get the point. Yet *I* have a point, too: When we live in fear, inspiration is virtually impossible.

Consider what I'm writing here with an open mind. In fact, let me offer this disclaimer: Every bad thing that's come your way, including any victim status, natural devastation, sickness, or what have you, *is not your fault*. There's no blame—you're not getting targeted for some kind of "karmic payback"—rather, what happened is there and it's yours. Since fear is a vibration, you were a vibrational match to whatever entered your life at the moment of its arrival. Remember that you live in a Universe that operates by the Law of Attraction, so when you live in fear, you actually bring to you what you're afraid of. Thoughts themselves are an energy, and it's vital to realize that you need to work at not holding on to the ones that will weaken you. Keep in mind that *you get what you think about, whether you want it or not!*

There's no fear in our spiritual Source—still we're persuaded to be afraid by continual exposure to the onslaught of fear-based dispatches that arrive on our doorstep. It's possible that our life experiences, which were a vibrational match to our thoughts at the time of their arrival, instilled fear in us. Nevertheless, this doesn't make our dread acceptable if we're dedicated to living in-Spirit. Franklin Delano Roosevelt was right: "The only thing we have to fear is fear itself."

Our Universe is created out of love, kindness, peace, and well-being, so when we're an energetic match to this awareness and refuse to live in fear, we'll attract the protection and guidance we desire. We can absolutely affirm that we won't attract anything that's harmful to us or to our loved ones, we can heighten our awareness that we're never alone, and we can have faith that whatever we need to experience is on its way and God won't send us anything we're incapable of handling.

We can also be aware that the word *fear* is just an acronym for **f**alse **e**vidence **a**ppearing **r**eal! That one phrase can help us remember that the ego is the false self, and identifying with it leads us to believe the false evidence. Even now, after reading all of this, some readers may continue to make fear real with thoughts such as, *He wouldn't be able to say these things if he knew all that I've been through.* But in my heart I know that this is a Universe that's on purpose and supported by a Creator Who is good. I never doubt it, and not only do I refuse to live in fear, but I also refuse to attract to myself the vibrational energetic equivalent of those fear-based thoughts. As an old German proverb proclaims: "Fear makes the wolf bigger than he is."

4. Sarcasm. Just about every situation comedy on television has a familiar focus: dialogue that's dedicated to sarcastic, unflattering comments between the supposedly comedic characters. Put-downs are the very bread and butter of almost all prime-time shows today, so in essence we're asking to be amused by children being smart-alecks toward their parents and siblings mouthing off to each other with as many disparaging comments as possible. Oh, and these nasty rejoinders are followed by a laugh track to really drive home that we're being "entertained."

Sarcasm designed to inspire laughter sends a message to viewers that's anything but inspirational. Remember, our ultimate calling is always about being in harmony with our Source of Being—we're all here as the result of a Creator Who has great respect for all of Its creations. Since no one is inferior in our Creator's eyes, no one deserves to be ridiculed for the purpose of gaining an artificial laugh . . . not in life or on TV. When a comment is made in jest and there's a kind of clever banter taking place, that's comedy at its best—but when hostility and disrespect are uttered in almost every verbal exchange, with the express purpose to discredit and mock another person, that's a decidedly uninspiring signal being sent to the audience. Awareness and choice are ours to exercise, so if this tendency toward sarcasm has become a habit, we must begin exploring alternatives to this style of entertainment and family interaction.

You may recall that I wrote earlier in this book about my mother—well, I simply cannot even imagine using her as the butt of a joke to demean or ridicule her. And yet I see this kind of disrespect taking place in nearly every episode of every situation comedy on the air today. Being courteous to others is a matchup to the energy of Spirit. Having fun, telling jokes, and being playful with others are all part of being in-Spirit, but a hostile, sarcastic sense of humor is an energy that moves us away from Spirit and into the realm of hurt and dishonor.

Cultural and Family Influences

I'd be remiss if I were to leave out this important category in this chapter. After all, we encounter lots of people in our everyday lives who attempt to convince us that we can't live the dream that beckons us. Statements such as, "That's not possible," or "We've never done it that way in our family," characterize our family or community members' attempts to dissuade us from following our calling. I've written about these family and cultural pressures in other chapters of this book, but they bear repeating here.

We need to be on the alert so that we're instantly aware of what others are trying to accomplish with uninspiring pronouncements about what we can or cannot do. Practicing increased awareness when we're around uninspiring family and/or cultural messages concerning our unique inspiration is extremely important: With that awareness, we're gracefully able to smile and politely move away from any energy that isn't encouraging us to follow our inner spiritual convictions to return to Spirit.

Many of our cultural influences are very subtle and aren't actually intended to be a distraction from our calling. Often, though, organized religions will push us in the direction of fearing God and living life in ways that have been prescribed by ancient theological doctrines and customs that have no merit in today's world. And frequently there are rules meant to quell desires that we may have to live out the life that we feel burning deep within us. In these situations we must look within, consult with our Creator, and make a decision to be in-Spirit—even if it conflicts with what we're being told by well-meaning people and institutions whose mission includes keeping us "in the herd."

Institutions of formal education may also want to discourage any attraction we have to listening to our inner guidance. This makes sense, since school is often designed to teach students to unquestioningly accept what's taught and to conform to societal standards. There's little room in this kind of classroom for following our own inner callings—the choice is generally between being like everyone else or being labeled as a troublemaker. Once again, we're forced to contemplate the Shakespearean dilemma of "to be or not to be." The stronger our burning desire to live a life of inspiration, the more we're pushed in the direction of "to be." We can learn to look at social pressures to conform and smile kindly, all the while choosing Spirit rather than the herd.

As I sit here writing, I'm looking at a framed photo of Ralph Waldo Emerson, a powerful man of Spirit and one of my most inspirational teachers and mentors. I'd like to end here by sharing an observation he once made: "Every man takes care that his neighbor shall not cheat him. But a day comes when he begins to care that he does not cheat his neighbor. Then all goes well. He has changed his market-cart into a chariot of the sun." This is a thought well worth pondering as we move in to the next chapter.

Some Suggestions for Putting the Ideas in This Chapter to Work for You

— When you find yourself being exposed to media onslaughts that are decidedly uninspiring, listen to your very first impulse and *switch off!* Turn off the television or radio, leave the movie theater, put the magazine down, and affirm: *I no longer wish to be in the energy field of anything that isn't a vibrational match with Spirit.*

— Be aware of brazen attempts by pharmaceutical companies to profit off of your presumed maladies, with advertising telling you to consult your doctor for some new medication. Let the ad be a reminder that you're an instrument of health; by doing so, your body will react to the messages being sent by your mind. Remember that your body/mind is the greatest pharmacy ever created. It has an unlimited potential for creating well-being, since that's where it originated from in the first place!

— Say it out loud! By this, I mean, that you shouldn't be afraid to make unusual or provocative affirmations. For example, you might avow: *I won't attract any further illness to my life. I'll never allow myself to feel old, feeble, or frail; and I refuse to allow Alzheimer's, cancer, or any other infirmity into my life. I don't vibrate to frequencies that are designed to keep me from being in-Spirit.*

— Always remember that you're a being who was created out of love. Write this out, place in a conspicuous place, and repeat it to yourself: *I live in a Divinely inspired Universe. I have nothing to fear. I trust in myself, and when I do so, I trust in the very Wisdom that created me.* Convince yourself (as I have) that when you live on purpose and "take care that [you do] not cheat your neighbor," then you're watched over by a "Senior Partner" Who knows that you're both living and vibrating to the same spiritual frequency.

— Work at developing your faith each and every day by taking time to be quietly in conscious contact with the Creative Source of your being. When you take time to meditate and commune with Spirit, not only will you feel revitalized, but you'll adopt a defense system that can't be penetrated by efforts to uninspire you, no matter how frequently others may attempt to do so. Ultimately, you'll find that you won't even bother to invite uninspired energy into your life via the media—or any other source, for that matter.

* * *

On every radio, CD player, and television set there's a wonderfully inspiring little button that says *on/off,* and it's your choice to befriend it. You can literally push it anytime you wish, or you can use an inner off button whenever you're bombarded by anyone or anything whose purpose is to distract you from your ultimate calling to inspiration.

Don't be afraid to use the off button—it works!

CHAPTER 13

INSPIRATION
IN ACTION

*"In our era, the road to holiness necessarily
passes through the world of action."*

— DAG HAMMARSKJOLD

*"Knowing is not enough; we must apply.
Willing is not enough; we must do . . ."*

— JOHANN WOLFGANG VAN GOETHE

WHEN WE FEEL INSPIRED, we're on the "road to holiness"
that Dag Hammarskjold refers to above. Yet that road can only be
paved with actions that mirror the intention of our originating
Spirit—actions that we're capable of choosing consciously, if we're
aware of the duality of giving and receiving.

Like two sides of the same coin, giving and receiving are in-
separable. Other examples of our duality abound: Before we can
take a breath, we must give a breath; in order to give anything
away, we must first have been willing to receive it; and our ability to feed others is linked to being able to accept food ourselves.
Who has ever seen a person with a front but no back? How about
an inside without an outside? Or a magnet with a north pole but
no south pole? So, just as the Prayer of St. Francis reminds us that
it is in giving that we receive, in order to receive inspiration we must
be willing to give it away, and vice versa.

Two Examples of Inspiring Action

As Goethe instructs, reading a book about inspiration isn't enough, and certainly waiting for it to fall from the heavens into your lap won't work either! Clearly, if you want to be inspired, you must be willing to offer inspiration. You've got to act on a desire to inspire others, thus becoming a person of inspiring action yourself. So in this section I'd like to share two beautiful examples of inspiration in action with you, along with suggestions for applying them to your life.

Example #1

I was inspired by a short documentary called *Ryan's Well,* about a young Canadian boy whose actions made a huge difference in the lives of some people in Uganda. You see, as a first-grader in the small town of Kemptville, Ontario, Ryan Hreljac learned that there were people in Africa who didn't have clean drinking water—yet it would cost just $70 to build a well that could provide pure, potable water for an entire village. This six-year-old boy began a campaign to earn the necessary money, only to discover that the cost was actually several *thousand* dollars. His reaction was, "I'll do more chores" . . . and he did.

In the film we see Ryan travel to Africa with his parents a few years later. The villagers greet him with enthusiasm and declare a day of commemoration that they call "Ryan's Day," in appreciation of his commitment to helping his fellow human beings on the other side of the world. It turns out that Ryan was instrumental in helping to raise what eventually grew to be more than *a million dollars!* His inspiration had motivated other schools in Canada to get behind his project; after the national news media picked up on the story, the television networks climbed on board, too.

Here was one small boy who decided to act on his strong inner calling to help others. He had no money or other resources at his disposal, but he *did* have a burning desire to reach out and serve people in need. He was willing to do the chores necessary to fulfill his call to be a vibrational match with his Creator and serve others. In turn, his actions created an immense wellspring of inspiration for all who contributed and got involved in Ryan's foundation. He inspired the children in Uganda (and even the government and school officials in that country), who all paid tribute to the spirit within Ryan that did so much good (God) in a remote village far away from his small community in Ontario. Ryan himself was the recipient of even more inspiration than he gave away.

When I watched the film, I was so moved that I insisted that all of my children see it, and they became inspired as well. In fact, I'm writing these words with the admitted intention of inspiring others to take action, too. Ryan's Well Foundation has a Website (**www.ryanswell.ca**), and with some inspired action, everyone reading these words can find their way to it and contribute to making clean drinking water, something most of us take for granted, available for others.

One person's inspiring actions will ultimately lead to many, many others. In the duality of inspired actions, giving and receiving inspiration is a never-ending circle of living more and more in-Spirit.

Applying this example: The moral of Ryan Hreljac's story is that none of us has an excuse for not being a person of inspiration. We don't need money or the help of any government or bank—all we need is an internal commitment to be more like God, and then to act on that desire. Everything else that we need will begin to arrive when we're in-Spirit: The right people will show up, the financing will materialize, those around us will be attracted to our enthusiasm and commitment, and we'll be a source of inspiration to others . . . while becoming more inspired ourselves.

Ryan's story represents our true nature, and our ability to be purposefully in-Spirit. He found a way to give to others the inspiration he wanted for himself, and all those who observed this boy in action responded in kind. To that end, whatever *we'd* like in our life that would provide us with inspiration is there—we just need to find a way to offer to others what we desire, and we'll solve the riddle of how to feel inspired and give inspiration away at the same time.

Example #2

On a recent airing of *Extreme Makeover: Home Edition,* Cassie, a young cancer patient, was given a surprise by the show's producers: They built a beautiful mansion where the tiny bungalow that housed the little girl and her large family once stood. But Cassie hadn't written to the show to ask for a more impressive home for her family; instead, she wanted the producers to consider making over the children's cancer ward in the hospital where she spent a large portion of her young life. She felt that the surroundings were far too dreary—the walls were bare, and the entire place was disheartening—and she felt that a makeover would help uplift and inspire everyone, including her young friends who were also patients. The show agreed to finance and re-create the children's cancer ward, and they also got all the kids involved in the project.

When it was completed, the ward looked like a fairyland that any child would love: Playrooms replaced old storage closets, the walls came alive with creative artwork, and the sleeping facilities were redone so that they no longer even resembled hospital beds. The entire ward turned into a place of inspiration . . . all thanks to the dreams of a very young child who listened to Spirit and took action. But I haven't even gotten to the most inspiring part of the story yet!

Without exception, all of the children in the cancer ward who participated in the renovation had their white cells increase in the direction of well-being and away from the damaging cancer in their bodies. Imagine—by moving more into harmony with Spirit and using this newfound inspiration to take action in the service of other children, the actual process of returning to perfect health was activated. The healing power within these young people somehow miraculously responded to the results and actions of Cassie's inspiration by increasing their white cells!

Applying this example: There's so much to ponder in Cassie's story—above all, how taking action to inspire others may activate something that reconnects us (and them) to a stream of well-being and perfect health. Additionally, there's the inspiration that we receive by giving. Consider these powerful words of Robert Frost, one of America's most illustrious poets: "Something we were withholding made us weak. Until we found out that it was ourselves." Our weaknesses, including our illnesses, may come to us because we're withholding something—which could very well be our healthy, conscious connection to Spirit. By taking action to inspire others in any way, we gain the opportunity to convert a weakness to a strength.

If a child of five or six who's living with cancer in a ward with other kids in similar circumstances can find a way to take action that inspires others, then surely *we* can go within and find our way to inspiring action. Little Cassie was acting more like God than ego when she wrote to the *Extreme Makeover: Home Edition* show. And she also behaved in a more God-realized way when she got involved in the cancer-ward renovation to make it a more healing and good-feeling place. As one of my greatest mentors and teachers, Carl Jung, once observed: "Whatever you do, if you do it sincerely, will eventually become a bridge to your wholeness, a good ship that carries you through the darkness." Dr. Jung's key advice centers on the word *sincerely*, which I interpret to mean "in collaboration with our essential spiritual essence." By taking action from that place of Spirit, we become whole again, and all darkness dissolves.

Cassie and Ryan's examples are not out of our range, no matter who we are or what our place in life is. We *all* have the capacity to become inspired, to act in a more God-realized fashion—we just need to take the time to seek out the opportunities to do so.

How *I've* Practiced Inspiration in Action

In this section, I'd like to present some examples of my own deliberate efforts to put the duality of inspiration in action into practice. I work at this every single day of my life: Every human encounter represents a moment of truth for me, one in which I choose to be reconnected to Spirit and offer to others what I genuinely want for myself. The opportunities present themselves in the form of a smile or a greeting or an extension of kindness, even if it's just a silent blessing to a person begging on a street corner or a prayer said quietly to myself when I hear a siren. (The siren is a reminder to me to offer my thoughts of comfort to whomever is in need of assistance.) These are habits that I've developed over a lifetime.

Then there are the days when I go out on a premeditated odyssey of inspiration, without any fanfare or need for recognition. Here's the result of one such inspiration excursion—and keep in mind that this all happened in one afternoon!

— I reside on west Maui while I'm writing, and on this particular day I decided to make the 20-mile trek to Costco to load up with supplies for two weeks of uninterrupted writing. As usual, someone was standing by the roadside looking for a lift to "the other side." This is a commonplace occurrence here on Maui, and it's my regular practice to pick up whoever's seeking a ride—usually a young person with a surfboard or a couple with luggage needing transportation to the airport. I always view giving rides as an opportunity to serve another person, and I get to feel good as well. If you're thinking about how dangerous this practice might be, I simply don't ever entertain such thoughts, and I never attract people or events into my life that cause me harm. It's just not my way of being in the world.

On this day I picked up a 41-year-old Canadian named Raven (Maui tends to attract people with names like that) who needed to get to the airport. As we talked, it turned out that my passenger hadn't spoken to his father in 17 years, distancing himself out of respect for his mother and sister, who had their own unresolved conflicts with the man. Raven admitted that he felt distressed and incomplete; moreover, he found himself repeating some of the behavioral patterns of his father's that had caused this family rift in the first place.

I brought up the subject of forgiveness, mentioning this quote from *A Course in Miracles:* "Certain it is that all distress does not appear to be but un-forgiveness." I related the story of my experience at my own father's grave in 1974, and how that one single act of forgiveness turned my life around and headed me back in the direction of Spirit.

As I dropped Raven off at the airport, he hugged me. With tears in his eyes, he said, "I can't believe how much this one trip has changed my life. I feel that you were sent here by God to remove this sword that's been hanging over my head. I know what I have to do, and I will do it soon." It was a moment of inspiration for both of us.

It would have been just as easy for me to maintain silence on that 20-mile ride along the ocean, but I knew that on this day, I was on a pilgrimage of inspiration, and Raven was one of my co-conspirators.

— I headed back to Costco for one of my favorite activities. I love the opportunity to purchase large amounts of goodies of all description in the store's open, warehouse atmosphere, among lots of local people doing the same thing.

At the back of the store on this day, a gentleman who recognized me from my PBS appearances approached me and wanted an appointment to discuss a problem he was having. I informed him that I was writing a book, so a scheduled meeting would be impossible. But knowing that some force had brought us together in the midst of all this delightful chaos, I asked, "What's the problem?"

The man told me that he was a diabetic who'd developed a fail-safe method for delivering insulin, in a manner that would leave no one out. "So what's the problem?" I once again asked. "Why not implement your plan?"

He went on to explain how he'd been unable to get the necessary government agencies to meet with him—various layers of bureaucracy were impeding his progress. On and on he went with a litany of obstacles that he felt were being placed before him, until I finally stopped him. "I sense that you know exactly what's needed, since you're a diabetic, too," I said. "And you know exactly what needs to be done to implement your idea."

He lit up like a Christmas tree. Giving me a knowing smile, he said, "Exactly, but I can't—"

I stopped him cold, reminding him that when we focus on what we don't want, then that's what we'll get. We get what we think about, whether we want it or not. I then asked him to consider staying out of the "system of obstacles" altogether; he should go ahead with his plan, forget about what couldn't be done, and just do it without the assistance or resistance of anyone else. "If your plan is viable, then they'll ultimately come along," I reminded him. "Just do it, and stop trying to get the approval of a bureaucracy." And then I asked, "You know what to do and how to do it, don't you?"

"Yes, I do," he replied, "and I will. I feel as if this little meeting was arranged by God just for me today." After getting my second hug from a "stranger" in the past 30 minutes, the man pushed his shopping cart away with a newfound sense of inspiration. He'd returned to Spirit, where the idea of anything being impossible is . . . impossible! And I'd been able to extend some Spirit offerings to another.

— Continuing on my way back to west Maui, I picked up a young fellow named Andy who was on his way to the Hard Rock Café. Fancying himself a Rastafarian rap artist, Andy had long dreadlocks and a strong inclination toward using marijuana as a stimulus for his music. As it turned out, he simply wanted to approach the manager at the Hard Rock to see if he could perform there on weekends. He was out of funds and without a plan—even his upcoming spontaneous audition had been purely a fantasy, since he hadn't contacted anyone at the restaurant for an appointment.

As we talked, I told him a story that my daughter Sommer had recently related to me. She has a little dog named Joey that she takes with her every day as she trains horses and gives riding lessons. Her friend Mimi had told her that Joey was a perfect example of a being at peace with God, and my daughter agreed. "Joey's mantra is: *Breathe in, breathe out, life is good,*" she said. "That's Joey all day, every day: *Breathe in, breathe out, life is good!*" Andy loved this story . . . so I asked him to give me a song using this theme as the primary lyric.

My car was suddenly filled with the sounds of a Rastafarian rapper pounding out a fast-paced lyric. It was sensational, and Andy was in heaven. By the time I dropped him off at the restaurant, he had his audition all planned, and he'd written his very first song: "Breathe In, Breathe Out, Life Is Good."

I handed Andy a $50 bill, which inspired him to cry out in appreciation, and off I drove. It was a double dose of inspiration: Andy was aligned with Spirit by being a creator of his own music and feeling purposeful and confident, and I was experiencing heaven on Earth for being able to extend love and assistance to another person. And it was my third such gift in the past two hours!

— Next I proceeded to a grocery store to pick up a few items in smaller quantities than were available at Costco. As I stood in the check-out line, I struck up a conversation with the woman behind me on the subject of raspberries. I was purchasing two half-pints of these precious little jewels to put on my morning bowl of cereal, and the lady asked about the price, which I hadn't noticed. She went on and on about how much she loved raspberries, but their cost was so outrageous—she'd never spend that kind of money, even for something she loved so much.

I responded by telling her about my happy memories of growing up in Michigan and picking berries as a young boy. To this day, raspberries are one of my very favorite foods, and I buy them whenever they're available. The woman could relate to my memories, since she grew up in Pennsylvania and used to pick the berries herself, coming home with red stains on her fingers and all around her mouth.

At the register, we saw that the baskets of berries came up as $7.99 each. My new friend almost collapsed, but told me to "savor each and every one of those little treasures." As I walked away, I reached into my bag and placed one of the containers in her hands and told her to enjoy them as a gift from me. This lady, who was counting out her change to pay for a single container of yogurt, was stunned. I finally convinced her that if she wouldn't accept them as a gift from me, she'd be depriving me of my own treat in knowing how much pleasure she was going to have relishing and savoring these little gems.

My new friend was obviously inspired by this unexpected expression of kindness to a "stranger." I could see the gratitude and love in her eyes as she tucked the berries in her straw bag. I, of course, was right on track, enjoying my fourth occurrence of inspiration in action on the same afternoon. And much to my surprise, number five was evolving right in front of my eyes. . . .

— In almost every aisle of the grocery store, I'd seen the same woman, dressed in flowery slacks and a bright orange blouse. As I approached the bakery to buy a loaf of olive bread for my daughter Serena's arrival the following day (she loves this bread!), the woman in the colorful outfit talked to me about a multigrain bread that *she* absolutely loved. "It's the best I've ever tasted," she said in a heavy foreign accent. As I approached the cashier, there she was ahead of me, asking if I'd hold her place while she picked up some item she'd forgotten. Then in the parking lot, she stopped her car to allow me to enter the exit ramp. Finally, as I was driving home, I spotted her again! Her car was sitting by the side of a putting green—with the door open and the engine running—and she and a man were hitting golf balls on the green.

To me, this was more that a series of accidental encounters, so I decided to turn around and deliver a present to her. I pulled up behind the car and approached with an autographed copy of *The Power of Intention* in my hand. It turned out that this lady was originally from Poland and was on her honeymoon. She introduced me to her husband, and I gave them the surprise wedding present, for which they were most grateful. I have no idea what took place in their lives after I drove off—I can't tell you why she kept appearing over and over again, or if the book I gave them made any kind of a difference in their lives—all I can say for certain is that these newlyweds were very touched by my gesture, and I had my fifth gift of feeling connected to Spirit in one afternoon!

As you can see, countless opportunities to reach into the lives of others in an inspiring way arise every single day. We can either act on these momentary impulses and feel inspired, or we can ignore them and stay in our ego-dominated world. I choose to act, for it makes me feel creatively alive, connected to good (God) and everyone else in the world.

Taking action is how we increase our connectedness to Spirit. If we're heeding our ultimate calling, we must be willing to act on that mission. We may believe that inspiration is something that arrives in some mysterious way that's beyond our control—or perhaps we're waiting for God to send us motivational signs—but it's clearly best to rely exclusively on our decisions to act in ways that will intensify our awareness of Spirit.

Try this action plan for a few weeks and see if you don't feel more inspired than you've ever felt before.

Some Suggestions for Putting the Ideas in This Chapter to Work for You

— Before beginning your day, spend a few moments with God during the early morning. When you awaken, remind yourself, "These are my few moments with God." During those precious seconds, ask, reflect, feel the peace, and most important, extend your gratitude. I end my few moments with God every morning with this: "Thank You, thank You, thank You!"

— Upon awakening, decide to do something, anything, that will improve the quality of life for someone, without seeking any credit for yourself. (If you can do it before breakfast, great!) A letter, some flowers, a contribution, an unexpected plan to visit someone later in the day—do anything at all that will make someone else feel good (God).

— Overcome your inertia. Since to be inert is to be without action, agree to become a being of movement: Plan to exercise, make that call you've been avoiding, or write that letter. Just as the key to Spirit is movement, the key to health is circulation. Spirit is always in a state of creation, so commit to less lying or sitting around and more movement.

— Listen to your inner voice and promise that you'll take corrective action. For example, if you've been addicted to alcohol or drugs, overeating, or being a doormat, listen to that inner voice that begs you to be big rather than small, and take one corrective step. Just for today, throw the cigarettes away, pass on the sweets, walk around the block, or stand up for yourself. That inner voice is God pleading with you to rejoin Him in-Spirit by being pure, strong, and an instrument of well-being.

— Accept no excuses: Stop with the BS and be truthful with yourself, admit your flaws rather than defending them, and look in the mirror and talk to yourself honestly. Affirm: *I am a creation of God, and I am Divine. I've forgotten this, but now I'm not accepting excuses. I'm going to stop fooling myself and work at being all that I was destined to be.*

— Experience the apprehension and *do it anyway!* It's the doing that brings you to a new level of inspiration, so don't deny your fear. Allow the panic to come, and then move in the direction of facing it. Visualize the fear right in front of you. Stare it down and tell it how you truly feel and what you intend to become: "I'm stronger than you. I have my Creator here with me as a Senior Consultant, so I'm no longer willing to allow you to have dominance in my life. I'm scared, but I'm also taking action."

— Look for opportunities that you're going to create to feel inspired. In my afternoon of inspiration described in this chapter, I made a specific decision to act in-Spirit. It was my choice. I was seeking those situations, and if they hadn't transpired, I would have made them happen. Once you get proficient at manufacturing circumstances that allow you to be inspirational, you'll begin to see these situations materializing all around you every day.

— Finally, don't ever quit. Never give up on yourself or feel shame as a result of not fulfilling your objectives to be a being of inspiration. Every fall that you take is a gift, and every relapse is a glorious opportunity—after all, without them you can't manifest the energy to get to a higher place.

* * *

There it is—a blueprint for taking action to live from inspiration. These strategies, as simple as they may seem, will bring you to a new level of inspiration if they're just adopted one day at a time. But reconnecting to Spirit *can* all happen in one day—this day. As one of my favorite Chinese proverbs reminds us:

> *I hear and I forget*
> *I see and I remember*
> *I do and I understand.*

If you want to understand inspiration, it will require some doing. So remember what the Dalai Lama says: "If you want others to be happy, practice compassion. If you want to be happy, practice compassion."

I close Part III of this book with the simple yet profound words of Shakespeare: "Action is eloquence."

PART IV

CONVERSING WITH YOUR SPIRITUAL SOURCE

*"The greater the power
that deigns to serve you,
the more honor it demands of you."*

— SOCRATES

CHAPTER 14

YOUR SPIRITUAL SOURCE CAN ONLY BE WHAT IT IS

*"I cannot imagine a God who rewards and punishes
the objects of His creation, whose purposes are
modeled after our own—a God, in short, who
but is a reflection of human frailty."*

— ALBERT EINSTEIN

"We are—because God is!"

— EMANUEL SWEDENBORG

IMAGINE A WAREHOUSE FILLED, from floor to ceiling, with coconuts—and one of them believes and acts as if it were a raisin. "Raisin" hasn't a clue that it's a coconut, too, and the other coconuts haven't a clue that Raisin doesn't know it's a coconut. Get the picture? When Raisin wonders why it's all dried up and wrinkled, the coconuts don't respond, because they only see another coconut (albeit a crazy one). In order to get the warehouse coconuts to respond, the raisin will have to communicate as the coconut it really is. All coconuts, just like us, cannot be anything other than what they are.

If we continue our lighthearted coconut/raisin metaphor and apply it to our Creator, we can see that if we (and coconuts) can't be something we're not, then we need to avoid asking our Creator to be or talk as if It's something It's not. Please pay close attention to the words that follow. They're from *The Disappearance of the Universe* by Gary Renard (Hay House, 2004), a special-delivery agent of *A Course in Miracles:* "Because your idea is not of God, He does *not* respond to it. To respond to it would be to give it reality. If God Himself were to acknowledge anything *except* the idea of perfect oneness, then there would no longer *be* perfect oneness."

When we understand these words, it changes the way we approach God, Who can't and doesn't interact with ideas that are false. We can then begin to clarify our knowing that Spirit is true and ego is false by realizing that we must come to God in terms that are *of* God in our prayers and our discourses. We'll know that we need to put ego aside and make a new attempt to speak to our Source in terms of It. This can be a radical shift, especially if we've always approached prayer and making conscious contact with God from the perspective of ego.

Five Characteristics of God

Let's now examine the elements that most of us agree define the essence of our Creator, along with how they can help us sensibly approach Him.

1. God Is Love

We came from love, and we desire to return to that heaven while still on Earth. I repeat Emerson's appropriate observation that "love is our highest word and the synonym for God"—in other words, if we dwell in love, we dwell in God. If God is love and cannot be anything other than what God is, and we wish to have a dialogue with Him, then it seems to me that we come to our Source in love or we're wasting our time. God cannot and will not respond to unloving requests.

Unloving prayers, which originate in arrogance, hatred, or fear, are the work of ego, so they won't be answered. In fact, they won't even be *heard.* God's message is to love all people, without exception, so we can be in vibrational harmony with Him. As the Bible reminds us, "[W]e are all members of one body" (Eph. 4:25) and "Let everything you do be done in love" (7 Cor. 16:14).

Now the way to approach God for guidance and help with anything in our life is to do so from the vantage point of forgiveness—for any and all we perceive to have wronged us, and for ourselves. Think about it: How can we expect God to hear our request for help in improving a relationship when we have hatred in our heart because of supposed misdeeds and maltreatment? God, Who only knows love, will have no idea what we're talking about.

No matter what our religion, whenever we want to discourse with our Source of Being, we must do so without malice or hatred in our heart. In this way, we'll shift our vibrational energy to a frequency that harmonizes with the highest vibration in the Universe, which, of course, is that of Spirit. As Saint Francis instructs so simply, "Where there is hatred, let [us] sow love."

Love and forgiveness will then activate the dormant forces I wrote about in the opening chapters of this book—that is, the right people and events will materialize synchronistically. This is because we're in-Spirit, remembering that God simply can't help if we expect Him to hear anything other than love and forgiveness. As Martin Luther King, Jr., once said: "We must develop and maintain the capacity to forgive. He who is devoid of the power to forgive is devoid of the power to love." This seems to say it all.

So in the private, quiet, prayerful moments of asking for God's help, don't ask Him to help defeat others in any way; rather, pray: "Dear God, make me an instrument of Thy love. I want to be like You. I have forgiven them, and I have forgiven myself." And remember that there can be no forgiveness without love—and without love, there can be no way of being heard by our Source.

2. God Is Peace

One of the most-quoted verses in the Old Testament (which may also be my favorite biblical offering) is this: "Be still, and know that I am God." So a corollary of this might then be: "Be agitated and turbulent, and you will never know God."

In order to communicate with our Source, it's vital to recall that *It can only be what It is.* And what It is, is peace and stillness. After all, creation doesn't take place in a violent manner—it's actually calm and peaceful. That is, movement from the invisible realm of Spirit into the material world of form isn't a loud, chaotic, explosive process—it's actually done with no fanfare at all. In the time it takes to read this chapter, millions upon millions of new life forms will emerge into this world, all without thunderclaps or fireworks. This is because peace is all that Spirit knows.

Now, if we approach God in a panic or with a frenzied, fearful, overly anxious demeanor, He's not going to help. You see, when we commune with our Source in a way that reflects an absence of peace, we'll have these nonpeaceful beliefs continually reinforced. By holding on to our panic, we'll believe even more in the disorder that our mind and body are accustomed to. Furthermore, we'll leave our prayerful state believing that our petitions aren't being answered, and very likely blame God for creating and allowing war and the other evils that define the world. Yet blaming God for the absence of peace is like the coconut who believes it's a raisin blaming the other coconuts for its wrinkled, dried-up life. The "raisin" is living an illusion, and so are we when we blame God for the absence of peace.

Along with praying or communing with our Source with peace in our heart, we must "be still." This means taking time to get quiet before meditating, and also monitoring our breathing. As we exhale, we can train ourselves to let go of all of our nonpeaceful thoughts, and as we inhale, we can breathe in Spirit.

We can also ask Saint Francis to guide us. He had very little peace in his lifetime, but when he prayed, he knew what his Source was like. Saint Francis wanted to be in-Spirit, so rather than asking

God to deliver him some peace so that he could escape the disorder and chaos he saw all around him, he'd request, "Lord, make me an instrument of thy peace." In other words, Saint Francis knew that God was peace, so in his prayer, he asked to be returned to a state where he'd be like his Creator.

We can keep reminding ourselves that all of the nonpeace that's in the world is not of God, it's of ego . . . then we can ask to be helped back to His peace. This approach will attract the assistance we're requesting—it's all about matching up the vibrational energy of our desire for peace with thoughts and behaviors that are consistently *peaceful* with those desires.

3. God Is All-Inclusive

We won't be heard by, or receive assistance from, our Source if we're touting our separateness from our fellow humans. You see, when we seek special individual favors from God, or even when we seek to converse with our Source from this perspective, we're once again living an illusion. If God were to acknowledge our belief in separation, as Gary Renard suggests, perfect oneness wouldn't and couldn't exist. It's impossible for a Source that creates everyone (and therefore is *in* everyone) to even have a dialogue with someone who's harboring ideas of their specialness or separation from everyone else.

We must be in a space of loving everyone—more than that, we've got to see ourselves as *connected to everyone*—in order to get the attention of our Source. So we've got to make every effort to avoid any thought that sets us apart from another being, such as a request to defeat someone, to have more than anyone else, to win a contest, to receive special attention on a job application, or to be considered first among many. These kinds of thoughts simply won't be recognized by a Source that's in all of the people we're asking to be given preferential treatment over.

Similarly, the great folly of war is the incredulous ignorance of the nature of God. When our politicians ask God to bless America, for instance, and to help us kill more of our "enemies" and win, it's analogous to having our body engage in a war in which our legs and lower torso are fighting against our arms and upper torso. Our body consists of all of its parts, so any war between them would surely kill the entire body. The body, just like God, can't process any talk of separation.

In conversing with our Source (as always), we strive to be more like It. So we need to see ourselves as connected to everyone in the Universe as we enter into prayer. Then we can ask for guidance and assistance in summoning that All-Inclusive Spirit: "Make me an instrument of You. Allow me to see You in everyone I encounter. Help me to see myself in others and to extend first to them what I aspire to myself. I've noticed that this is how You are, and I wish to be just like You."

This is the kind of dialogue that activates the dormant forces I've spoken of. The key is getting past our ego-based idea of separation and instead seeing ourselves a part of the oneness of all. As Thomas Aquinas put it so succinctly: "True peace consists in not separating ourselves from the will of God."

4. God Is Abundance

Picture this: A group of one-gallon containers has the capacity to speak to each other. One of them wants to discuss its emptiness with one that's always known fullness. "Full Gallon" probably won't be able to relate to the quandary of "Empty Gallon," since no matter how much Empty Gallon experiences lack, Full Gallon won't be able to understand because it can't be anything other than what it is.

While this is a crude example, it nevertheless illustrates our predicament when we attempt to engage in a discourse with God, a Source that's only known abundance, and ask it to relate to and correct our perceived shortages. Trust me, God knows nothing of lack, and there's enough of everything to go around. All of God's gifts, including life itself, are given as freely and abundantly as oxygen, sunlight, and water.

As Saint Paul once said: "God is able to provide you with every blessing in abundance." So why is there so much apparent shortage in the world, including people starving and living in poverty, and millions of folks having the persistent problem of too much month left at the end of the money? Well, what I can say for certain is that God is not to blame—there's more than enough to go around. After all, we came from a place that knows nothing of deprivation, and we arrived on a planet that has the capacity to grow the food and slake the thirst of every one of its inhabitants many times over.

As a species, we human beings have brought the ideas of deficiencies and depletions of God's gifts on ourselves, largely by taking very un-God-like actions. God serves all of us, but our greed has made us forget others and focus only on ourselves. As a people and as individuals, we've brought lack to our lives, and we can only fix this deficiency by becoming more like our Always-Serving, Endlessly Abundant Spiritual Source.

The answers to the resolution of poverty and scarcity are readily available to us, and they'd be resolved tomorrow if we remembered that we're all *one* on this planet: We all share the same origins, and we all end up back in the same nonplace where we began. When we return to Spirit in our heart, our governments will align with this truth, and our leaders will emerge from in-Spirit consciousness.

We need to pray for the elimination of a perceived shortage and approach God in the style of Saint Francis with words that go something like, "Make me an instrument of Thy endless abundance," rather than asking God to fulfill something that's missing. In this way we can summon His energy back to us, rather than staying focused on what we don't have. If we focus our thoughts on lack, we'll only attract more of the same.

We need to start seeing ourselves as a vibrational match to the frequency of God's abundance. If our desire is to attract wealth and prosperity, then we must entertain prosperous thoughts that match our desire and that activate the manifestation process. And the dormant forces of abundance will come to life to help fulfill these desires.

5. God Is Well-Being

Spirit never has a fever and knows nothing of illness, so in my humble opinion, it makes no sense to pray or engage in a discourse with God from a perspective of asking to be healed—unless, that is, we have a firm understanding of what we mean by the word *heal*. If we mean "to overcome an illness or infirmity," then I feel that we're again violating the truism that nothing can be what it isn't, including God. As Ernest Holmes once wrote: "The will of God is always good," which means to me that disease, sickness, and suffering are not part of God's energy.

On the other hand, if we use the word *heal* to mean "reconnecting to our Source of Well-Being," then we're open to the potential of receiving assistance to overcome any infirmity. And that's how *I* use the word. I never ask God to help me get over a feeling of sickness. Even when I had a minor heart attack five years ago, I asked to be made an instrument of God's well-being. I acknowledged that my body had taken on non-well-being, be it from my lifestyle, diet, and habits; or the toxins I breathe in and out—whatever—it was not of God. It was of me in this physical world, and I prayed to be reunited to a stream of well-being. I knew that I was a piece of God, and that it was just as easy for Him to heal a cut on my finger as it was to restore my heart to a healthy state. Since I knew that God's healing power was within me, I just needed to help my body remember this.

Similarly, in a time of recent disharmony in my life, I found myself feeling sick to my stomach and unable to sleep—until I remembered that this experience was a gift to me. As I conversed with my Higher Power, I asked for guidance and visualized myself as a magnet, attracting plentiful well-being. And in this way, healing was virtually immediate.

In *The Amazing Laws of Cosmic Mind Power,* Joseph Murphy offers this magnificent advice on conversing with God when we're seeking to be healed:

Know that God loves you and cares for you. As you pray this way, the fear gradually will fade away. If you pray about a heart condition, do not think of the organ as diseased, as this would not be spiritual thinking. To think of a damaged heart or high blood pressure tends to suggest more of what you already have. Cease dwelling on symptoms, organs, or any part of the body. Turn your mind to God and His love. Feel and know that there is only one healing presence and power. . . . Quietly and lovingly affirm that the uplifting, healing, strengthening power of the healing presence is flowing through you, making you every whit whole. Know and feel that the harmony, beauty, and life of God manifest themselves in you as strength, peace, vitality, wholeness, and right action. Get a clear realization of this, and the damaged heart or other diseased organ will be cured in the light of God's love.

These words bear reading repeatedly . . . especially when you take into consideration that my damaged heart of five years ago is now completely healed.

Some Suggestions for Putting the Ideas in This Chapter to Work for You

— Before beginning any prayerful activity, make a note to keep in mind precisely what your Source is and is not. Ask yourself, "Am I asking God to be something that He is not? Am I expecting my Spiritual Creator to join me in my ego, which has truly **e**dged **G**od **o**ut?" This will allow you to stay focused on clearing the channel between you and Spirit, rather than putting out requests to a Source that can't relate to your ego-driven world. Remember, it's you who has left God, not the other way around.

— Begin all your conversations with Spirit with, "Make me an instrument of . . ." Then add "love," "peace," "joy," "kindness," "abundance," "well-being," or any other quality that you know in your heart defines the essence of the Holy Spirit.

— As you put forgiveness to work in your life, study the ideas expressed in the two following observations:

"If we could read the secret history of our enemies,
we should find in each man's life sorrow and suffering
enough to disarm all hostility."

— HENRY WADSWORTH LONGFELLOW

"Tolerance comes of age.
I see no fault committed that I myself could not
have committed at some time or other."

— JOHANN WOLFGANG VON GOETHE

Assimilating these thoughts will help you to practice forgiveness. We all have times in our life when we totally understand the common phrase "there but for the grace of God go I." Attempt to be that grace of God, and extend it to all you believe have wronged you.

— Make it a daily practice to meditate for peace—yours *and* the world's. By going within, you can make conscious contact with God. Then your Spirit energy will radiate to those around you, and to those on the other side of the world as well!

— Remember that the healing power of God is within you. That same power, which made your body, knows how to restore it to its original state of well-being. All you have to do is remove all of the obstacles erected by you and our toxic world, and allow this healing power to flow through you.

✵ ✵ ✵

Before we go on to the next chapter, let's go back to the observation made by Emanuel Swedenborg, "We are—because God is!" and add, "Not because of what God isn't."

CHAPTER 15

YOUR SPIRITUAL SOURCE KNOWS

*"It is true that Divine will prevails at all times
and under all circumstances. . . . There is no need
to tell God your requirements. He knows them Himself
and will look after them . . ."*

— RAMANA MAHARSHI

"The thing we surrender to becomes our power."

— ERNEST HOLMES

AS THE FATHER OF EIGHT CHILDREN, it goes without saying that I've witnessed many occasions when a two-year-old made a request that couldn't be accommodated. Often the request became a standoff, with the toddler crying, insisting, and even throwing a tantrum—but since I was the adult, I'd stand firm and refuse to grant the child's wishes. Running around the block unsupervised, racing through the house with a sucker sticking out of his or her mouth, playing with electrical sockets, climbing up the stairs alone, and putting his or her fingers in a younger sibling's eyes were some of the behaviors forbidden by me, the parent, who simply knew better.

If we put ourselves in the place of toddlers and give our Creator the very same leeway that we, as parents, took with our children, the purpose of this metaphor becomes perfectly clear. Just as it's absurd for a two-year-old to insist on having his or her way, our

Creative Spirit doesn't need to be reminded of what to do for us or how to go about doing it—It already knows. In fact, there's a wonderfully enlightening quote in the Bhagavad Gita that says: "Only the fool whose mind is deluded by egotism considers himself to be the doer . . ."

When we're about to enter into a discourse with our Creator, it's crucial to approach with the understanding that we aren't the doer. It may sound a bit extreme, but this is how Immanuel Kant described our situation: "God is our owner, we are His property; His providence works for our good." (Please don't take the word *owner* as an insult—it's only the ego that's offended by this concept.) In other words, we needn't presume to tell our Source what needs to be done to provide us with a happy, fulfilling life. Instead, it's our job to change our thinking so that it's vibrating to a frequency that matches God's energy. And this begins by understanding that it's impossible for God to forget *anything*. Unlike human parents, God is omnipotent, so it's unnecessary to remind Him of our needs.

Our Creative Source Never Forgets

When I lived in New York, I had a cat named Schlum. Every October and November I noticed that his coat would get thicker in preparation for the coming winter months—even though the current temperatures might be mild or even warm, Schlum's fur would be in the process of changing. I remember thinking about this fact and being in awe of the great Source of All Creation. There must be millions of cats, dogs, beavers, rabbits, rats, horses, and other fur-bearing animals living in the Northern Hemisphere who go through the same process every year—and our Source never forgets a single one of them.

One August when I visited a dingo farm in Brisbane, Australia, I was told that the wild dogs were shedding their coats for the upcoming spring. *Spring after August?* I thought, before remembering that the seasons follow opposite patterns in the Southern Hemisphere.

Wondering if this would be confusing to God, I asked the farm's curator what would happen if a dingo was shipped on an airplane to New York in August—would its coat go from thinning to thickening, since winter would now be following summer?

"Happens all the time," the curator said. "We fly them up there, and when they arrive, their coats start to thicken up." Amazing, isn't it? Now, if God remembers to adjust the coat on a dingo flying on a 747 from Australia to New York, surely He doesn't forget us!

All of our life experiences—the struggles, the falls, the victories, the lessons, the emerging talents, all of it—is orchestrated by our Source. Be mindful of this fact: Whatever we decided upon with our Creator in advance of our manifestation into form is playing out right now. We must strive to always consciously remember that God hasn't forgotten us—even though we may have edged God out—because He *can't* forget us.

Just as all that composes decomposes, our infinite self is only here for a few moments in eternity. But even though we're on loan for this temporary human experience, we're never ever forgotten by God, the Source that provides us and everything else that lives and breathes with the energy to sustain life. So we need to continually trust that the organizing intelligence of our Source, which is always operating in the Universe, is ever-mindful, and provides us with every blessing in abundance.

Trusting and Surrendering

Now how do we trust a Source that we can't see or touch? Well, we can start by noticing the results that we attribute to It and tell ourselves, "Someone or Something is responsible for all of the ongoing infinite creation that I witness with my senses, and I'm going to trust in It from now on." This is the kind of logic that I hope I've been conveying throughout the pages of this book—that it's possible to reconnect with where we came from, and where we came from isn't physical (as our quantum scientists now inform us). But rather than using blind trust or my attempts at logic to trust in the existence and the assistance of Spirit, I suggest that we ultimately each use our own life experience for our "trust barometer."

Returning to the analogy at the beginning of this chapter, most children are free-spirited little beings who don't think about questioning their parents' judgment. After all, mothers and fathers tend to know what's in their offspring's best interest, including what's required for successful survival. These senior partners look out for their kids' needs and direct their early life activities—and they do this as long as is necessary, which is usually until their children begin to develop the ability to trust their own instincts and apply what they've learned.

As adults, we can look back on our earliest days with a strong sense of appreciation: We learned not to play in traffic, to avoid eating poisonous foods, to get enough rest each day, and so on. Today we feel thankful and appreciative that our parents were there to guide us toward the responsible, self-contained people we are now—we can appreciate that they did what was best for us, and they never forgot us.

I trust that the analogy is clear: Our relationship with God, our All-Knowing, Never-Forgetting Senior Partner, is just like our childhood relationship with our parents. Just as we did with our mothers and fathers, we're now choosing to trust in the wisdom of our Creator. In other words, we don't need to be told by virtual parents what's best for us, and we don't have to rely on so-called religious superiors to keep us in line because we're no longer needy little infants. We now trust our Source because we've matured to a point where doubt has been supplanted by faith. Somewhere between childhood and maturity, we surrendered and trusted our parents, just as we're now surrendering and trusting the All-Knowing, Loving Source of Creation.

Surrender in Southeast Asia

By beginning the process of turning our life over to a Higher Power and staying connected to Spirit in inspired living, we become more observant and less attached to our ego-driven beliefs and attitudes. A lifesaving example of this came out of the devastating tsunami of 2004, in which 305,000 people either died or were reported missing. This gigantic tidal wave affected people in Indonesia, Southeast Asia, and even as far away as the shores of Africa.

Months after this tragedy, reports came of a nomadic tribe of people who lived on the water, traveling back and forth between a series of remote islands off the coast of Thailand. Their villages and boats had been destroyed, yet they suffered not a single casualty—it seemed like a miracle!

It turned out that these people had a history of orally passing down the wisdom they'd gained while living on boats and on secluded islands that were far removed from modern civilization. They'd lived on the water all of their lives, as had hundreds of generations of their ancestors. Because they lived so closely with nature, they knew the water and how to catch fish with crude wooden spears, but mostly they stayed connected to Spirit. And they relayed what they learned from generation to generation.

Tribal elders had passed down stories of tsunamis in ancient times, so when one of them noticed a sign of the shifting water patterns in 2004, he immediately knew what was coming. As the beneficiary of ancient knowing, he alerted everyone on the boats and in the villages to move to higher ground immediately. No one doubted his wisdom—everyone, without exception, left their boats and villages and moved to higher land. When the tsunami hit, it destroyed every boat and home, yet the entire tribe safely watched from a distance as the water did what they knew it was about to do.

I believe that these nomadic people survived because they lived lives defined by being in-Spirit—there were no words indicating ego consciousness in their language. They lived in God-realization, grateful for all that they were given; consequently, they were able to join in God's knowing and make it their own. I suggest that we can do the same, even while living in a world where so many have chosen to be in-ego rather than in-Spirit.

Just as the tribe in Southeast Asia surrendered to their Spiritual Source and permitted ego to stay out of the picture, we too can become more observant and aware of what we need to do when we're in-Spirit. We just need to stop believing that we're the doer, and instead learn to listen to and trust our inner intuition—which, of course, is guiding us in collaboration with the creative power of the Universe.

Communing with the All-Knowing

Imagine a camera that can accomplish photographic feats that no camera has performed prior to this time. For instance, it can take pictures through concrete walls, or in the dark without benefit of a flash. But most ingeniously, it can record a person's thoughts, producing an exact pictorial likeness of what any subject is imagining at the moment the shutter snaps. And inside the camera's package is an invitation to talk with the creator of this remarkable device. The printed material states that he'll be happy to discuss how and why his invention works, along with the amazing results that it can produce.

The conversation we'd have with the creator of our new miracle gadget probably wouldn't begin with the things we thought he'd forgotten or should or shouldn't have done. And it's unlikely that we'd complain about the price or how it was marketed, or attempt to convince him that we had more expertise. Instead, we'd probably use the opportunity to maximize our ability to work with our new camera and derive the greatest pleasure possible as it performed the tasks it was designed to accomplish.

It's safe to say that we'd approach the creator of something we can see, touch, and use—but haven't a clue as to how it came into being—with deference, respect, and awe because we'd be so eager to absorb all that he has to offer. If this analogy is unclear, you might want to quit reading at this point and seek an expert to remove your blinders! Clearly, I believe that we should approach our Creative Source with openness, and the willingness to maximize our ability to be in-Spirit.

When we finally "get" that our Source is all-knowing, we can approach the act of spiritual communication from an entirely egoless perspective. Our discourse must begin with a recognition that it's impossible for us to be ignored. We can link up to all-knowingness by thinking like God—that is, by being an energetic match in our thoughts and actions, by being grateful, and by thinking of others and offering them what we desire.

Since we know that when we ask, it is given, we must next ask God for what we want. I'm not implying that we should beg, or think that we've been overlooked, but rather ask in a way that takes the form of a vibrational shift in energy. So we'd request to be an instrument of God's abundance, for instance, instead of pleading for cash. We'd simply match what we want with the All-Encompassing Abundance that is our Spiritual Source.

Note that any- and everything that keeps us from appreciating our Spiritual Source is an impediment. This particularly includes relying on someone else or some organization without examining the truths that they insist we believe. While this may come as a surprise, Jesus wasn't a Christian, Buddha wasn't a Buddhist, and Mohammed wasn't a Muslim. These were Divine spiritual beings who came here as emissaries of truth . . . yet when their truths were organized, we saw the horrors of inquisitions, mass murders, crusades, holy wars, and jihads, all in the name of "God."

Those who claim to represent these Divine beings of truth frequently do so from a decidedly nonspiritual perspective. When an organization includes some, yet excludes others, they're announcing that they're not actually preaching or teaching truth. Since God excludes no one, any religious organization that does isn't affiliated with Him. God is all-knowing. *No one else is,* unless they experience pure God-realization . . . and those beings who have ever lived among us belong to a very small club.

No one else can intervene for us in our efforts to commune

with our Source of Being: We shouldn't rely on organizations, gurus, rituals, temples, or any other outside sources as the means to make conscious contact with God. Instead, we must approach the All-Knowing Source in silent communion, and be willing to listen and receive guidance. We must speak in words of our own choosing with statements that tell God: "I know that You are all-knowing and could never forget me. I desire to align with Your all-knowingness, to have the faith that I can attract into my life all the goodness, peace, and abundance that You are. I will stay in this place of trust, for I am here to serve. I am grateful for all that You are, and all that You allow me to be."

Co-creating with Spirit

Keep in mind that we can't co-create with anyone, including our Spiritual Source, unless we're in a place of harmony. To that end, we must suspend our false self (ego) and stop all thoughts of resistance before we can participate in creating the inspired life we desire, in perfect symmetry with Spirit. Whatever we ask of our Source in our prayerful communion will no longer be a wish or a hope—it will become a reality in our mind, just as it is in the mind of God. The how and when of its arrival, which have always troubled ego, are no longer issues.

We maintain our optimism with thoughts such as *I desire it, It's in harmony with my Source,* or *It's on its way—there's nothing to fuss about.* And then we can relax and surrender to our knowing. As Ernest Holmes reminds us: "The thing we surrender to becomes our power." I know that the term *surrender* is generally associated with defeat, but there's no victor or victim when surrendering to God—this isn't about winning or losing.

You see, what we're doing here is giving up our false self in favor of returning to our authentic one. And when we do, we'll meet our Spiritual Creator and become empowered to live in the same vibration with It. We'll become co-creators by surrendering and joining the All-Knowing, All-Creating Force that allows everything to come into existence. Then our knowing replaces our doubts, and "Divine will prevails at all times." Only now, *we* are in harmony with that Divine will.

Some Suggestions for Putting the Ideas in This Chapter to Work for You

— Put some of the well-known words of the recovery movement to practical use in your life. *Let go and let God* is a wonderful phrase to repeat to yourself when you feel under pressure, overly taxed, frustrated, or just plain angry. By saying these words, you'll free yourself to allow the only real Doer there is to take over, and you'll become an observer rather than feeling the futility of trying to control things. Try it now. Let go and let God . . . relax into the awareness that you have an All-Knowing Partner. Now what's there to worry about?

— When you begin to question God's omniscience, banish that doubt from your mind. Shakespeare reminds us that "Our doubts are traitors / And make us lose the good we oft might win / By fearing to attempt." Notice that he says "lose the good," which is another way of saying "lose the *connection to God.*" In other words, your doubts keep you from joining in God's knowing. Think about it: How can you know and doubt at the same time?

God knows, and you want to be like Him in order to be inspired. So when you communicate with God, do so from your own knowing that He is there, listening and ready to spring into action with you.

— When you pray or otherwise communicate with your Creative Spirit, don't assume that just because It's all-knowing, It's going to handle every problem for you. Remind yourself that you're a co-creator, and you have the free will to choose to either be or not be consciously connected to that Creative Spirit. When you consciously surrender to the *co* in co-creator, it will assist you in a zillion mysterious ways.

— Here's a suggestion from one of our great commonsense ancestors, Mark Twain: "Keep away from people who try to belittle your ambitions. Small people always do that, but the really great make you feel that you, too, can become great." Your ambitions are of God, so as you communicate with Him, ask for the strength to ignore those around you who'd malign or otherwise disparage what you and your Source have placed in your heart.

— Remind yourself as frequently as you can that to surrender is a sign of enlightenment and strength. What you're surrendering to is responsible for all of creation—it's to this omniscience and omnipotence that you're surrendering, and it's here that you'll gain your power to live an inspired life.

* * *

Many years ago I copied down this observation by the brilliant Ramesh Balsekar, an enlightened scholar. I still ponder this frequently, and I feel that it concisely sums up what I've written about in this chapter: "Most of the near-perfect actions or performances, and almost all the works of creativity, happen in this state of egolessness, when the tenet 'Thy will be Done' is actually put into practice."

As you pray to the All-Knowing Source, it only makes sense to close your communion with these four words: *Thy will be done.* But keep in mind that *Thy will* also includes you.

CHAPTER 16

IT'S ALL ABOUT
REMEMBERING

"The memory of God comes to the quiet mind.
It cannot come where there is conflict; for a mind
at war against itself remembers not eternal gentleness. . . .
What <u>you</u> remember <u>is</u> a part of you. For you must be as
God created you. . . . Let all this madness be undone for you,
and turn in peace to the remembrance of God,
still shining in your quiet mind."

— FROM *A COURSE IN MIRACLES*

I HOPE YOU'VE GATHERED BY NOW that becoming inspired isn't achieved by attending workshops, learning new techniques, or by following a master teacher—it can only be accomplished by returning to Spirit, or going back to a place where we experienced bliss. After 15 chapters emphasizing this point, there shouldn't be any doubt that we originated in love and peace from a spiritual Creator.

This chapter is going to focus on our communication with God from a perspective of remembering Him, rather than trying to befriend some spiritual presence we don't know. That is, we need to tune our prayers and discourses to help us recall who we really are and what it was like before we came to this physical world.

Most of us will probably find it difficult or even impossible to recollect what we abandoned so long ago when we adopted ego as our self-definition. But this picture of eight-month-old Tysen Humble (one of my grandchildren) in a bathtub has to inspire anyone looking at it to see the relevance of remembering.

What a joyous creature in rapturous harmony with life! Tysen's expression reveals pure and complete bliss, and just looking at him is enough to make us smile—especially when we think about what *we* surely must have felt when we were his age.

This beautiful baby also communicates something to us about ourselves: As we remember our Spirit, we want to keep in mind Tysen's state of jubilation and absolute contentment. It isn't just a smile and a burst of laughter that's responsible for that blissful expression on my little grandson's face—there's an invisible force coming through what we see in the photo, and that's what we want to return to. If we could see our Spiritual Source with our eyes, we'd witness pure joy, ecstasy, happiness, and peace—the photo you see on the previous page is a personification of that. It's also important to note that we emerged from the same vibrational energy as Tysen, and we had the same inner sensation that's unmistakably evident on that baby's face. It's denied to no one.

If we train ourselves, we can recall feeling the bliss that's on my grandson's face and which inspires his entire persona. *Everything* we've ever experienced is still stored as an invisible memory, and we can access it if we choose. For example, when my grandmother was close to death and doing what some called "involuntary hallucinating," she was pulling out all kinds of facts from her earliest days. Street addresses; the names of neighbors; locations of family outings; relationships with friends of her own mother, who were only there in my grandmother's infancy—all of it was somehow available to her. It turned out that in some mysterious way, Grandma was tapping in to memories that everyone else thought couldn't possibly be recalled because she was only a baby at the time.

I have no idea how she did this—all I know for certain is that we reach into our own personal history and bring to the present thoughts that impact our state of mind as well as our level of inspiration. You see, the mere recollection of something in the past that we call a memory is capable of affecting us either positively or negatively in the present moment; therefore, they're extremely powerful tools for our current state of mind. Obviously there are some negative memories lurking around somewhere in the nethermost regions of our mind, but why access them if they're going to cause us to feel uninspired? Instead, let's think about how to get back to that delirious happiness that's portrayed by the gleeful Tysen, who's only a few months removed from 100 percent immersion in the rhapsodic arms of his original Creator.

What I'm trying to make clear here is that we've got to figure out how to return to where we came from in order to commune with our Spiritual Creator. Therefore, being inspired itself is going to require us to go back and do some major remembering.

Remembering Your Spirit

At the beginning of this chapter, there's a powerful quotation from *A Course in Miracles* that I feel sums up all we need to know to facilitate going "all the way back"—that is, prior to our baby days, our birth, and even our conception. It's about remembering our origination. I committed this passage to memory many years ago, and I use it as a way to remember who I truly am and where I really came from, particularly when I communicate with my Creator to stay on purpose and in-Spirit.

Now I'd like to go through each of the messages in this observation from the *Course* one by one:

1. "The memory of God comes to the quiet mind." We came from a quiet, peaceful place that's the very essence of creation, so when our mind is filled with noisy dialogue, we shut out the possibility of remembering our Spirit. Incessant chatter keeps us attached to the physical world and produces anxiety, stress, fear, worry, and so many of the emotional reactions that are decidedly removed from God-realization.

A quiet mind is open to recall because it allows us to open a space within ourselves where we experience a sensation of familiarity with Spirit. Intuition sharpens, we access higher energy, and what we thought of as information about God is supplemented with an unmistakable remembrance. Knowing *about* God is very different from actually knowing God—so a quiet, disciplined mind is needed to be able to remember, and consequently return to, a state of being in-Spirit.

We must minimize distractions when we wish to communicate with God, so being in nature, away from the artificial noises that invade our space, is helpful. But the most important thing to consider is how to keep our mind free from the dizzying, bewildering cascade of thoughts flowing through our head from morning till night, and even on into our dream state. It's been estimated that we have something like 60,000 separate thoughts every day.

The real problem is that we have the *same* 60,000 thoughts today that we had yesterday!

I've made the practice of meditation a part of my daily life because it's one way to quiet the mind so that the memory of God is accessible. So by learning to meditate—or at the very least shutting down the inner dialogue produced, directed, and acted upon by your ego—you can open up a space for remembering and returning to Spirit.

2. "It cannot come where there is conflict . . ." In order for conflict to exist, there must be two opposing forces at work; that is, one force—in the form of an idea, a point of view, a desire, or a contribution—directly clashes with another. Conflict defines our lives in many ways, as we oppose our partners, our children, our bosses, our neighbors, and even our countries. In politics, it's always one party versus the other, and the entertainment industry portrays battling points of view that are usually turned into violent scenes. Essentially, conflict requires "two-ness."

However, remembering where we came from involves our returning to the oneness of being in-Spirit. After all, there are no battling powers in the Divine realm of Spirit—there's only perfect oneness, and this is what we want to rejoin. We want to become one again with our Creator, and we can't retrieve this "memory of God" with a mind in conflict in any way.

Imagining oneness is often a difficult process because we're so steeped in our beliefs of two-ness and dichotomies. If God (Who is perfect oneness) was able to acknowledge our beliefs in conflicts and two-ness, then oneness simply could not exist. So we need to leave all conflict out of the picture to succeed in remembering God and achieving oneness. In our mind's eye, this is done by picturing ourselves fully integrated with our Source. Visualizing melting into the oneness of God will lead to a sense of merging until we can no longer make a distinction between ourselves and Him. And this consolidated state is where our memories of God become luminous and unobscured.

3. ". . . for a mind at war against itself remembers not eternal gentleness." Conflicting thoughts tend to fill our consciousness with never-ending chatter, including plans for retaliation against those people we label as the source of our discontent. It's not at all uncommon to conduct an imaginary dialogue that goes something like this: "First I'll say this to her. Then when I say that, she's going to respond with this. But she always says that, even though I know she's lying. So this time I'll trip her up by responding this way. She'll have to agree that I'm right—but she never does. I know that I'm right, and I'm going to force her to admit it. I'll tell her that even her own mother agrees with me. . . ." This could go on all day and night, and it frequently does. We conduct this inner combat over and over again—and the only advantage is that we almost always win the argument being waged because it exists only in our mind.

The second part of this teaching from the *Course* reinforces that a combative mind cannot remember where it once resided in eternal gentleness. Obviously you can't wage war and simultaneously focus on peace and gentleness, and it is eternal gentleness that you want to remember and rejoin. It's really quite simple to do this: Just close down the battlefield and surrender. Remove all of the artillery, send the soldiers home, and replace the instruments of war in your mind with thoughts of peace, tranquility, and surrender. Making your mind a place of peace is achieved by your own will, so steadfastly refusing to have thoughts of conflict allows you to activate the glory of remembering your Spirit.

I can recall times in my life when I've cluttered up my mind with that back-and-forth inner dialogue with my children or my wife. I'd literally get to a point of exhaustion by silently repeating my side to their side and back again, until one day I made the decision to abandon this battleground in my head. I began to practice putting the word *cancel* up on my inner screen, and I'd stubbornly refuse to go through those senseless sparring matches in my own mind. After a few days of practice, it became my automatic response to go to eternal gentleness—and peace and Divine guidance were my rewards.

4. "What *you* remember *is* a part of you." Every memory I have is me . . . what a glorious feeling it is to know this! We each have the power to retrieve any piece of ourselves that we desire, and to experience it right here, right now, in this present moment. The great Danish theologian Søren Kierkegaard once observed that "life can only be understood backwards, but . . . it must be lived forward." In other words, if we can't go back and remember the spiritual bliss that defined us before the beginning, we've abandoned a part of ourselves.

As we move into communion with God, we must know that our inability to remember our spiritual origins is another way of saying, "I'm unable to know myself because I have no recollection or memory of my Spirit." In fact, the corollary of this line from *A Course in Miracles* that we're processing right now would be, "What you *don't* remember is *not* a part of you." In other words, if we fail to remember Spirit, then obviously it isn't a part of us.

The most effective thing we can do to remember our Source is to affirm unhesitatingly: *I'm first and foremost an eternal spiritual being—I can't be anything but this. I will never doubt it, and I can go within and try to be like God in all of my thoughts and actions.*

When we begin this inspirational practice, the memory of our spiritual origins will emerge from behind the clouds and become unquestionably clear.

5. "For you must be as God created you." I've made the following point repeatedly throughout the pages of this book: *We must be what we came from.* Just like that droplet of blood must be like the rest of our blood supply because that's what it came from, we must be of God because that's what we came from. It's only by **e**dging **G**od **o**ut that we've come to believe that we are our false self.

As you communicate with your Source of Being, know that you're awakening a part of yourself that's just like God. In fact, you ought to try to approach communication with God by being as closely aligned to the way that you were created as possible—that is, by becoming a vibrational match to the All-Loving Creator. Come to the quiet moments in consultation with God in love, in peace, and without judgment. As the *Course* is saying, you must be as you were created—so why put on a false mask and pretend to be anything or anyone else? In this way, you can open the channel of communication because you've finally remembered to be the way you were created—and that's the key to effective prayer. And, as Gandhi once said: "Prayer is not an old woman's idle amusement. Properly understood and applied, it is the most potent instrument of action."

6. "Let all this madness be undone for you, and turn in peace to the remembrance of God, still shining in your quiet mind." Let's take the three suggestions in this teaching one at a time.

— First, the *Course* says to "let all this madness be undone." The madness here is that of living in a state of conflict. In other words, we must make an attempt to transcend the dichotomies of our life because the division creates so much suffering and keeps us from living an inspired life. I remember a Ram Dass lecture in which he said, "I've firmly come to the conclusion that there are no 'thems' for me anymore. I can't be told who to hate, who to fight, who to subdue—I only see an 'us' in my heart."

All those messages to divvy up our world are insane. All our self-centeredness just drives our ego's insatiable appetite for making us special and putting other people down. All our inclinations toward violence—even when it's "acceptable," such as supporting war in the name of patriotism or endorsing hatred in the name of doing our duty—are wrong. The *Course* encourages us to be done with this madness once and for all, both in our mind and in our actions.

— Second, we're told to "turn in peace to the remembrance of God." Once again, we know in our heart that we came from a place of peace, so any discord can't be the result of our Creator's actions. God cannot come to us when we pray from nonpeace, so the solution is to return to the remembrance of Him and ask to be made an instrument of His peace. When I find myself out of sorts, I remember. And what I remember is to turn to peace right now in prayer. I become peace, rather than anguish, and I feel the calmness I long for come over me like a wave of pleasurable relief.

We always have the power within us to shift into a peaceful mode. And when we respect someone, we're able to be in peace in their presence by suspending our inclination to be arrogant. For example, I recall watching John McEnroe behave in boorish ways on the tennis court, slamming his racquet, hurling profanities at the referees, and generally being in a very nonpeaceful state—but he never behaved this way when he played his rival, Björn Borg. Amazingly, McEnroe was almost always able to control his outbursts of negativity whenever he played this cool, easygoing, nonviolent, brilliant tennis player. Because he respected Borg so much, McEnroe came to his presence in peace.

— Finally, the *Course* reminds us that this peaceful remembrance is "still shining in [our] quiet mind." Notice the words *still* and *quiet*—regardless of where we are in life, if we're breathing we're connected to our Source of Being, even though the connection might have gotten a bit corroded. We still have the remembrance of God shining inside of us . . . it can't be otherwise. Our job is to access those memories, and it will help if we keep them in our *quiet* mind. This remembrance doesn't shine in our ego mind, our noisy mind, in our self-important mind; rather, it shines in a quiet, nonviolent, peaceful, loving mind. When we go to the quietness, that shining is a luminous reminder of how to approach our Creative Spirit by remembering.

One of my favorite teachers is the Russian mystic Leo Tolstoy. In his powerful book *The Kingdom of God Is Within You,* I was struck by the words he used to implore his 19th-century readers to heed nonviolence in their war-torn country:

> If you believe that Christ forbade murder, pay no heed to the arguments nor to the commands of those who call on you to bear a hand in it. By such a steadfast refusal to make use of force, you call down on yourselves the blessing promised to those "who hear these sayings and do them," and the time will come when the world will recognize you as having aided in the reformation of mankind.

What Tolstoy is saying is that it is incumbent upon all of us to return to the peace from whence we came. We must refuse to use force, especially in our thoughts—and above all, we must remember our Spirit.

Some Suggestions for Putting the Ideas in This Chapter to Work for You

— Find a picture of yourself as a very young child in which you were lost in your bliss. Place that photo in a conspicuous spot and let it serve to remind you that the same Spirit you're expressing in the photograph is alive and well within you right now, and that you're going to remember it and consort with it every day.

— Train your memory. By doing so, you'll be able to return to early childhood memories of love, peace, and joy—and back even further to your spiritual origination. Recapturing early events in your life will help you discover that you have more access to your past and your spiritual beginnings than you might have believed. It's all in there, so discipline yourself to become a retriever.

— Pray in solitude. Make peace with silence and remind yourself that it's there that you'll come to remember your Spirit. As Blaise Pascal, the great French scientist and philosopher, once remarked, "All man's miseries derive from not being able to sit quietly in a room alone." When you're able to transcend an aversion to silence, you'll also transcend many other miseries. And it's in this silence that the remembrance of God will be activated.

— Vow to have fewer conflicts in your life. It is your objective in reading this book to become inspired—therefore, you'll want to bring a halt to your feeling that conflict is normal and unavoidable. You came from no conflict, and you can return to that heaven right here on Earth by refusing to have your inner world conflicted by anyone at anytime. Affirm it over and over: *I do not attract conflict to myself.*

— Try this visualization that I replicate here from *The Book of Runes:*

> *Visualize yourself standing before a gateway on a hilltop. Your entire life lies out behind you and below. Before you step through the gateway, pause and review the past: the learning and the joys, the victories and the sorrows—everything it took to bring you here.*

By doing this exercise, you'll be practicing the virtue of remembering, and it will almost force you to return to Spirit!

* * *

You don't have to learn a single new thing in order to communicate and make conscious contact with your Source—it's all in you already. All you have to do is remember. . . .

CHAPTER 17

THE LANGUAGE OF SPIRIT

"When asked where God is, people point towards the sky or some far and distant region; no wonder then that He does not manifest Himself! Realize that He is in you, with you, behind you, and all around you; and He can be seen and felt everywhere."

— Sathya Sai Baba

IN THE PREVIOUS THREE CHAPTERS I've tried to stress that it's our job to take responsibility for opening the channel to communication to God, rather than viewing Him as a "cosmic bellboy" whose job it is to listen to our whims and respond just because we asked. But how can we recognize when our Spiritual Source is getting in touch with *us*?

Spirit's messages are not necessarily going to be in our native tongue, since It is in no way restricted by words (either written or spoken) as the exclusive means for communicating with us. Remember, the world of Spirit contains the highest and fastest energy in the Universe—it vibrates so quickly that it manifests the invisible into particles and then into the forms that we see, touch, taste, hear, and smell with our senses. All It needs is to activate the immensely mysterious power of creation and send us guidelines and assistance via its high-energy vibrations.

As Jesus said in one of my favorite quotes (which I've shared thousands of times in my life): "With man this is impossible, but with God all things are possible" (Matt. 19:26). I'd like you to read through the ideas I'm offering here concerning the language of Spirit with this quote in mind. As weird as some of the communication patterns I talk about may seem, and as much as your ego may be tempted to dismiss them as mere coincidences and devoid of meaning, remember that "with God all things are possible."

We're communicating with a Source Energy that creates worlds, One that knows no restrictions and certainly doesn't use the low-energy, slow-language methods that we do. Spirit communicates instantaneously, tapping in to our higher faculties of intuition, telepathy, insight, psychic awareness, spirit acumen, clairvoyance, the sixth sense, and even beyond.

The brilliant poet Rainer Maria Rilke put this all into perspective when he made this observation: "We must accept our existence *to the greatest extent possible;* everything, the unprecedented also, needs to be accepted. That is basically the only case of courage required of us: to be courageous in the face of the strangest, the most whimsical and unexplainable thing that we could encounter."

Being Ready for the Teacher

It's been known for millennia that "when the student is ready, the teacher will appear." Well, our teachers are always there because they're gifts from Spirit. The real question is our readiness to tune in to what they have to teach us. The key word here is *readiness*—that is, we must be open to all possibilities and trusting in our intuitive hunches.

Wondering if something might possibly be a message from God is evidence that we're open to our intuiton. Our thoughts are sacred and substantiate our connection to the Divine, so they don't need to be corroborated by anyone or anything else. Our Creator is listening and responding in ways that don't necessarily correspond to the laws of the material world—that is, we won't be hearing from a physical source that's aligned with cause and effect, the laws of physics, or even what we believe is "possible." It's our job to do all that we can to vibrationally match to that spiritual energy.

We were once perfectly together with our Creative Force, and now we're being called to come back to It. It's vitally important to be open to the language of alignment—most of us need to begin the process by recognizing our tendency to discount such messages as mere happenstance. In an infinite Universe, with an organized intelligence supporting it at all moments, there can be no such thing as accidents.

For the rest of this chapter, I'll be offering some of my own hunches about how the All-Knowing Creative Spirit communicates. Some of these ways fall into the category of "inexplicable alignments," which means that there's meaning there, but our ego mind—chained as it is to its belief in the material laws it has always lived by—refuses to see the hidden messages that are staring us right in the face.

The Four Messages of Alignment

For many years I've felt what I considered to be the language of Spirit speaking to me in ways that often defy my logical mind. These feelings are more than hunches and even go beyond intuition—and I sincerely believe that they've contributed to my living an inspired life.

The following four examples aren't rules or laws that apply to everyone, but if they *do* work for others, I'll be even more inspired because it's my intention to be in a space where I'm able to give to others all that I know. I also offer these ideas with the constant reminder that when one listens to Spirit, all things are possible. (And even though I'm offering them in a numbered sequence, they certainly don't conform to any linear arrangement.)

1. Alignment of Feelings

When I feel good (God), I'm aligned with Spirit. As I tell my children, we must rely on how we feel to determine our state of health, rather than seeking our answers in a medical printout full of numbers. Feeling energized, content, excited, and happy are better indicators of our health and well-being than having our bodily functions assessed by a distant laboratory. A positive honest response to the question, "Does this [or will this] make me feel good?" tells us immediately if we're aligned with our Creative Source or not.

For example, I'd been having an uninspired relationship with my cell-phone provider. For weeks I'd been unable to resolve the conflict: Each morning I'd plunge ahead and call the company again, traipse through the endless recorded messages, be on hold for sometimes a half hour, and finally reach a supervisor who'd read this from a company manual: "We're doing our best and apologize for any inconvenience this may be causing you. We can't give you a timetable for when this will be resolved."

Every day I'd hear the same words being read, so it was obvious that I was getting nowhere. But what upset me more than this lack of progress was my unmistakable misalignment. I was so upset I wasn't feeling good that my writing, my exercise program, and even my health were being negatively impacted. And then I remembered to follow my own advice.

The next time I started to go through my morning ritual with the cell-phone company, I stopped and told myself that I intended to feel good on this issue. I then put the phone down, went for a swim in the ocean, and thanked God for a renewed sense of peace. And sure enough, a voice inside me said, "By not being able to receive your calls, you've been given a rare opportunity to be at peace, which is something you've complained about in the past because of so many disturbances. Also, the phone company is doing the best they know how, so surround them with light and let the issue resolve itself." And finally, the most astonishing thing I heard was, "You're being protected from receiving messages that wouldn't serve you well. I have put your incoming calls on temporary hiatus so that you can be free from what will only make you feel bad. So enjoy your peace!"

I've since allowed Spirit to handle the issue, and now when I think about what was such a source of annoyance and inner turmoil for me, I feel good (God). This might seem like a petty example in a book about such a large topic as inspiration; nevertheless, I urge you to ask the question, "Does this make me feel good?" and pay attention to the answer the next time there's a similar "petty" situation in your life. You may be surprised to find yourself realigned!

2. Alignments with Nature

Everything in nature is in-Spirit—it isn't spoiled by ego, nor can it ever be. So when nature speaks to us, we should listen intently. When a wild bird touches us, for instance, or a fish brushes by when we're swimming in the ocean or a lake, I believe that it's a direct communication from our Source of Being. Since these creations of God instinctively keep their distance, when they depart from their DNA patterns to actually contact us physically, I think we should pay attention.

A few times in my life, I've had a bird sweep by my body, and on each of these occasions I've felt a deep sense of connection to God. Each time I've stopped and reexamined my thoughts at the precise instant of contact, and I was able to interpret that connection as a message to pay closer attention to my mission of writing.

Just today, as I walked along the ocean and thought about writing this section on nature and spiritual alignment, a bright red cardinal flew within inches of my face and stopped right in front of me. It looked directly at me, nodded its head, and flew off, again very close to my body. At the time of this encounter I was contemplating whether to even include these bird stories, considering that they might be misunderstood or perhaps even criticized by the professional community. In such moments, I always decide to listen to my own inner knowing—let the critics be damned!

I also recall other ways in which nature has gotten my attention and let me know that I was in touch with Spirit. For example,

I remember once being in a fierce wind and having a leaf blow right into my face, almost smacking me as I was thinking a decidedly nonspiritual thought of revenge; on another occasion while I was filled with anger, a tree branch collided with me as I exited my car—and it was a calm day without a breeze, and nothing was visibly disturbing the tree. And I have a piece of driftwood that meandered into my open hand while I was meditating at one of the "Seven Sacred Pools" near Hana (on Maui). When it touched me while my eyes were closed in deep meditation, I was startled— yet I knew that it was saying something to me. This wood, which I've kept for more than 22 years, is a reminder to me that Spirit is alive and working. To this day, when I look at it I think of God . . . and as you know, thinking of God and becoming like Him are precisely what it takes to live a life of inspiration.

Pay attention to episodes in nature that arouse Spirit and kindle an inner spark of awe and admiration for you. You don't have to discuss it with another being—if it has meaning for you, it's valid. (In fact, this is the first time I've shared the story of my sacred piece of driftwood.) Listen to the winds, the critters, the clouds, the rains, and the oceans—listen to it all.

Here's a Chinook Blessing Litany that reveals the Native American awareness of the language of Spirit inherent in all of nature:

We call upon the earth, our planet home, with its beautiful depths
and soaring heights, its vitality and abundance of life,
and together we ask that it:
Teach us, and show us the way.

We call upon the mountains, the Cascades and the Olympics,
the high green valleys and meadows filled with wild flowers,
the snows that never melt, the summits of intense silence,
and we ask that they:
Teach us, and show us the way.

We call upon the waters that rim the earth, horizon to horizon,
that flow in our rivers and streams, that fall upon our gardens

and fields, and we ask that they:
Teach us, and show us the way.

We call upon the land which grows our food, the nurturing soil,
the fertile fields, the abundant gardens and orchards,
and we ask that they:
Teach us, and show us the way.

We call upon the forests, the great trees reaching strongly to the sky
with earth in their roots and the heavens in their branches,
the fir and the pine and the cedar, and we ask them to:
Teach us, and show us the way.

We call upon the creatures of the fields and forests and the seas,
our brothers and sisters the wolves and deer, the eagle and dove,
the great whales and the dolphin, the beautiful Orca and salmon
who share our Northwest home, and we ask them to:
Teach us, and show us the way.

We call upon the moon and the stars and the sun, who govern
the rhythms and seasons of our lives and remind us that we are
part of a great and wondrous universe, and we ask them to:
Teach us, and show us the way.

We call upon all those who have lived on this earth,
our ancestors and our friends, who dreamed the best for
future generations, and upon whose lives our lives are built,
and with thanksgiving, we call upon them to:
Teach us, and show us the way.

And lastly, we call upon all that we hold most sacred,
the presence and power of the Great Spirit of love and truth
which flows through all the universe . . . to be with us to:
Teach us, and show us the way.

Indeed, nature has much to teach us, and it *will* help show the
way. All we need to do is align with its perfection and note how it
aligns with ours.

3. Alignment with Events

Strange occurrences and seemingly inexplicable events may actually be our All-Creating Source lining up "coincidences" to teach us and show us the way. Recently, for instance, I'd been advised to read a particular book that had been on bestseller lists for several months. I looked for it in various stores at the airport, but finally gave up because it was time to board my flight.

The title was still swirling around in my thoughts as I got to my seat. A woman who'd had her seat changed twice ended up sitting next to me, and she was carrying the very book I was seeking. And when I got home and turned on the TV, a guest on a talk show was talking about it. I couldn't help but notice the four alignments within a few hours concerning this book: my friend telling me about it, my search for it in the airport, a fellow passenger reading it, and a talk-show discussion of it.

When I experience these kinds of alignments, I've learned to not dismiss them as accidental. I'm still not totally certain of what was happening here, but I did purchase the book (*The Secret Life of Bees,* by Sue Monk Kidd), and while reading it I happened upon a story that I quoted in *this* one. Perhaps all the aligned events showed up so that the message in that story would be read and shared by someone reading this work, or so I'd have this example—the possibilities are endless!

One of my favorite quotes is from Mark Helprin's *Winter's Tale:* "In the end, or, rather, as things really are, any event, no matter how small, is intimately and sensibly tied to all others." It's exciting to observe the pattern of events appearing repeatedly in our conscious field of experience. We can notice the spine-tingling amazement we feel while reminding ourselves that this could very well be Spirit inviting us in to reconnect with It.

The language of Spirit will proclaim its creativity by producing sequences of repetition to align us with our Source. When we have an idea about taking on a new project and then read about it in a magazine that mysteriously shows up in our hands, and then a stranger in line at the movie theater begins talking to us out of the blue about this same topic—which is mentioned in the movie itself—and during dinner we overhear the people at an adjacent table discussing this same subject, guess what? We're in an "alignment attention-getter," written and carried out by Spirit. In other words, this is not an accident—the teachers are not only showing up, they're practically hitting us over the head!

The reason we begin to notice all of this aligned synchronicity is because we've tuned in to it. The teachers have always been there, but now we notice them. And our noticing indicates a new level of readiness to listen to our ultimate calling. In fact, these alignments can take some really interesting forms. The same numbers showing up—for example, we awaken at precisely 4:44 morning after morning, and then see those numbers appear on the odometer, on the radio, as a checkbook balance, at the deli counter, and as an assigned number for a charity walk—causes us to ask, "What's going on here?" The answer is that the Universe is asking us to be receptive and pay attention. It's not about playing all fours in a casino or the lottery—it's about knowing that these seemingly accidental repetitions are actually invitations from Spirit to join It.

Over the 30 years I've been writing books, I can't tell you how many people have told me, "A book just fell into my hands off of the shelf, and it was exactly what I needed at the time." I'd wager that virtually every person has had a similar experience more than once in his or her lifetime. (I trust in this type of spiritual communication whenever I write a book: I feel guided to pick up a particular item, and I know I'm in alignment with Spirit when these kinds of messages continually materialize throughout the months of preparation and actual writing.) When a book literally falls into our lap or is sent to us by several different people—or even when we keep seeing the title and having it referred to by others over and over—we need to notice, stop our resistance, and surrender. When we end up reading the contents and applying what it offers, we're aligning ourselves and becoming a vibrational match to the same Source that's sending us these signals.

4. Alignment with People

We commonly receive alignment when our thoughts become strangely tied to the actions of another human being. For example, we think about somebody we haven't seen for several years; in fact, we can't seem to shake our inner visions of him or her—especially when someone else mentions the same person for no apparent reason, or we run across a picture of that individual. Then the phone rings, and it's the same person whom we haven't been in contact with for years! The language of Spirit works by aligning our thought energy with the vibrational energy of another.

When people line up with our thoughts and mysteriously connect their physical presence with our private inner meanderings, we should take note. We must tell ourselves, "Spirit is aligning my thoughts with events that are happening. I'll stay alert to what I'm being offered here because there may be a reason." That's all—just be cognizant of what might be happening, and by being open to what may be baffling and perhaps indecipherable, we're likely to discover what we're being guided to learn.

A few weeks ago I was reading through a book I'd written 16 years ago. In it, I mentioned a friend, Earlene Rentz, with whom I attended school from fourth grade through high school. I put the book down and went jogging, yet Earlene was still on my mind. I thought, *I'm going to call her the next time I'm in Detroit—after all, we're both having our 65th birthdays this year.*

That very evening, I was scheduled to receive the Martin Luther King/Mohandas Gandhi Peace Award from the Unity Church of Maui, which would be attended by approximately 1,000 people. As I completed my speech and walked to the lobby to sign autographs, I saw the little girl who sat next to me in grade school, who was my first love, and who occupied my thoughts throughout my school years. Believe it or not, as I was thinking of her more than a half century later, Earlene was thousands of miles from home and hugging me in the lobby of a theater in Lahaina! It turns out that she was visiting Maui, had seen the award announcement in the newspaper, and had come to the auditorium to surprise me. It was one of those synchronistic alignments of Spirit at work. Somehow at an unconscious level, I was already reconnecting to Earlene without being aware that she was even in the area.

Noticing the same folks showing up in different settings; running into people we haven't seen in a while after we've just heard their names mentioned; and repeatedly seeing an individual's name in magazines, on television, or at a local bookstore are all also synchronistic alignments. Spirit is lining up these sequential happenings for a reason—we just need to be open to learning the reason, and it most likely will be revealed. Perhaps it will be a dream or a sudden instant of *Eureka!* or maybe it will become clearer when simply allowed—no matter how the message comes, we'll look back on it with a renewed insight and the benefit of no longer being closed off to such possibilities.

It may be helpful to consider that even with all of our sophisticated technology, we can't reproduce an eyeball that can compete with the ones made by our Creator. One little eyeball and we're all baffled! And our Creator's making them at the rate of six million per day—and that only takes *human* eyeballs into account! If a Spiritual Creator can do that, then aligning our thoughts with the people we need as teachers now is a minor task indeed. Again, with God, *all things* are possible.

Some Suggestions for Putting the Ideas in This Chapter to Work for You

— Always remember that when the student is ready, the teacher will appear. Stay in an attitude of readiness at all times, and the teachers and the teachings will manifest for you. Write or print out these words and place them in a conspicuous place: *I am ready.*

— Once you've declared your readiness, don't scoff at anything or anyone that may have some connection to your return to Spirit. Even an overheard conversation between four-year-old children can be a message to you—if it registers with you in any small way, then drink it in and allow yourself to process it as a Divine communiqué.

Trust your own intuition—no one else has to agree with you or even understand you. In fact, I'd urge you to resist defending your inner inclinations to anyone who has an attitude of resistance. Remember, you want to feel good (God).

— Now begin the process of actually looking for ways in which Spirit might be communicating with you right now. When these unexpected synchronicities appear (as they will more and more frequently when you're open to them), ask what it is that you're to learn from them. When you peacefully ask your Creator in quiet meditation or prayer, you'll see what it is that's guiding you. There are angels of Spirit surrounding you, so don't be hesitant to ask. And, of course, when you do, you will receive.

— Be prepared to make major changes in your life after you become accustomed to what these alignments you're experiencing are saying to you. I personally received many messages from Spirit that told me over and over that I was to give up my addictive ways—yet for years I ignored them at my own peril. Today I look back at the obvious nature of what I was being encouraged to do, and now I know why I had to ultimately follow those alignments of energy or die.

You may be guided to leave a job, a city, or even a relationship—all of which may sound terrifying at the moment. Nevertheless, if the signals keep coming and they resonate internally with you, take the step—and while doing so, know that you're being guided to a life of inspiration.

— Whenever you seem to be receiving an unexpected jolt from the Universe, make every effort to note precisely what it was that you were thinking at the moment you took in the message. That bird that touches you, that leaf that blows into your face, that toe you stub for the third time—anything at all—note your thoughts at the moment and see if you can detect any connection to what has just happened. Your thoughts are energy, and Spirit communicates by aligning Itself with you by getting your attention, and allowing you to then move on it or ignore it.

* * *

What I know for certain within my very core is that there's no separation between us and all that we encounter in the Universe. One of my favorite poets is William Butler Yeats, and here he perfectly sums up the ideas in this chapter:

> *O chestnut tree, great rooted blossomer,*
> *Are you the leaf, the blossom or the bole?*
> *O body swayed to music, O brightening glance,*
> *How can we know the dancer from the dance?*

You are the dancer and the dance, just as God is. In other words, those messages from Spirit are you if you feel them—because it's impossible to separate the dance from the dancer, the root from the blossom, and you from God. The only place where separation takes place is in your mind. But since you're now heeding your ultimate calling, you're right on your way to living an inspired life.

PART V

A PERSONAL
LOOK AT
INSPIRATION

*"There is a way of living in the world
that is not here, although it seems to be.
You do not change appearance, though you smile
more frequently. Your forehead is serene; your eyes
are quiet. . . . You walk this path as others walk,
nor do you seem to be distinct from them,
although you are indeed. Thus can you serve
them while you serve yourself. . . ."*

— FROM *A Course in Miracles*

CHAPTER 18

HOW LIFE LOOKS
WHEN I AM INSPIRED

"Give me a man who sings at his work."

— THOMAS CARLYLE

"They can because they think they can."

— VIRGIL

IN THIS FINAL CHAPTER, I offer my own very personal view on how the world looks when I feel inspired.

I'd like to acknowledge right from the outset that I don't live at this level of being in-Spirit 100 percent of the time—like most everyone else, I occasionally have lapses and feel uninspired. Yet these moments have become rarer and rarer; in fact, it's difficult for me to recall a day in the past several years when I felt completely uninspired.

What follows is a personal account of both how I feel inside and what seems to take place in the world around me when I feel connected to Spirit in the ways that I've written about in the pages of this book.

Jack

The same day that I completed Chapter 17 and read it over the telephone to my editor, Joanna, on Bainbridge Island, Washington, I had the most profoundly mystical experience of being in-Spirit in all of my 65 years.

When I finished up with Joanna, I went for my daily hour-long walk along the beach . . . but for some reason I elected to take a slightly different route along a grassy area *adjacent* to the beach. I was recalling my friend Jack Boland, a Unity minister in Detroit, who crossed over about a decade ago. Jack loved monarch butterflies, often telling stories of how he marveled at these paper-thin creatures who migrated thousands of miles in high winds and returned to the same branch on the same tree where they first emerged from their cocoons. Before Jack passed away, I presented him with a beautiful paperweight containing a dead monarch that I'd found in perfect condition. When he died, his wife returned it to me, telling me how much Jack loved that gift and how much he admired these amazing creatures who had such mysterious intelligence built into their brains, which are the size of a pinhead.

Jack always told me to "be in a state of gratitude," and he ended every sermon with this message to God: "Thank You, thank You, thank You." On three occasions since his death, a monarch butterfly has landed on my body. Since these creatures studiously avoid human contact, each time this has happened I've thought of Jack and thought, *Thank You, God—thank You, thank You.*

Anyway, as I walked, feeling grateful for having completed the second-to-last chapter of this book, a monarch landed on the ground, not three feet in front of me. I said Jack's magic words to myself *(Thank You, thank You, thank You)*, and felt deep appreciation for my life and the beauty of the day. The butterfly stayed right there until I approached, then he flapped his wings several times and flew away. Thinking of Jack and feeling a little bewildered and immensely thankful, I watched this creature in flight, now 40 or 50 yards away.

As God is my witness, the butterfly made a U-turn and not only headed in my direction, but landed right smack on my finger! Needless to say, I was shocked—but not totally surprised. I must confess that it seems to me that the more I stay in-Spirit, the more I experience synchronicities similar to this one. But what followed did border on the incredulous, even for me.

This little creature became my constant companion for the next two and a half hours—he sat first on one hand and then moved to my other hand, never even coming close to flying away. He seemed to be trying to communicate with me by moving his wings back and forth, and even opening and closing his tiny mouth as if attempting to speak . . . and as crazy as it may sound, I felt a deep affinity to this precious living being. I sat on the ground and simply stayed with my new fragile friend for 30 or so minutes. Then I called Joanna from my cell phone, and she was also stunned by the synchronicity, insisting that I somehow get a picture of this event.

At this point I decided to return to my home, approximately a mile from where I was sitting, with my new companion. I returned along the beach walk, where the winds were brisk—the butterfly's wings were pushed by these high gusts, but he clung to my finger, and even moved to another hand without making any effort to leave. As I walked, I encountered a four-year-old girl with her mother. The girl was sobbing over some perceived tragedy in her young life, and when I showed her my "pet" butterfly, her expression went from sad to blissful in one split second. She smiled from ear to ear and asked me all about the winged creature on my forefinger.

When I got home, I was talking on my cell phone to my friend Reid Tracy as I walked upstairs. He laughed with me as I related the bizarre synchronicity at play in this very moment. I said, "Reid, it's been 90 minutes, and this little guy has adopted me." Reid also encouraged me to get a photograph of this, since it was obviously in complete harmony with what I was writing.

I left my new friend—whom I was now calling "Jack"—sitting on the handwritten Chapter 17 on my lanai, and went downstairs. I found Cindy, a young woman who works nearby, and asked her to run to the store and purchase a disposable camera. She did, and I went back to the patio, put my hand next to Jack, and watched him jump right onto my finger!

It appeared that my butterfly companion had decided that he was now going to live with me forever. After another hour or so of meditating and communing with this little creature of God—and pondering this event as the most unprecedented and out-of-the-ordinary spiritual episode I'd ever encountered—I gently placed Jack back on my manuscript while I proceeded to take a long, hot shower. When I returned to the patio, I placed my finger near my winged friend as I'd done many times in the previous 150 minutes, but he now seemed like a totally different little critter. He fluttered away, landed on a table, flapped his wings twice, and flew off, straight up toward the heavens. Moments with him were now history, but I still have the photographs, which I treasure.

The next morning, I decided to watch one of my favorite films, *Brother Sun, Sister Moon,* which I hadn't viewed for more than a decade. And sure enough—in the opening scenes of Franco Zeffirelli's interpretation of the life of St. Francis, there he was . . . with a butterfly alighting on his fingers.

Inspirational Vibrations

When I live my life so as to be open to the language of Spirit, I find almost overwhelming rapture overtaking me. For several days after my experience with Jack, people kept telling me that I seemed so peaceful and content, and one woman even suggested that I was "walking grace." This episode with my butterfly friend and the communiqués from Spirit touched me at an unprecedented level. From the perspective of being in-Spirit, I've seen Its hands embrace me and heard It say: "You are not alone. You can count on Me to guide you—and whatever you do, do not doubt My presence."

This makes me feel safe, comforted, and that I'm not alone.

I feel good (God) because I'm living in almost perfect harmony with the Source of my being, living on purpose and writing from my heart. The reason I feel inspired isn't because the world looks perfect. Rather, it's the other way around: The reason the world looks perfect to me is because I'm in-Spirit—a person who chooses to live an inspired life. I'm able to stay in a state of gratitude from the moment I awake early in the morning right up until I close my eyes while falling asleep; and throughout each day, I'm reminded that staying in-Spirit is really about staying in vibrational harmony.

I don't find it necessary to change anyone or anything that I encounter or read about in my daily life. Each time that I'm tempted to, I catch myself and return to a mind-set that calls to me to be more like God, right here and right now. I stay inspired by making an energetic shift within myself; when I do, the world looks completely different, and I move inwardly toward peace and kindness. The energetic shift is merely a way of processing people and events from the insight of being unified with the All-Creating Source—that is, by eschewing judgment and allowing the world to be as it *is*, rather than as I think it *should be*.

I stay inspired by encouraging others to live out their destiny and allowing the world to unfold as it will, and I'm much more likely to feel peaceful. In fact, when I'm living my life from this perspective of inspiration, my vibrational energy is more attuned to that of the creative energy of the Universe, and I find that my effect on others is far more spiritually aligned. Furthermore, I know within my own being that I'm doing something very powerful to make this world a more spiritually oriented place for us all.

You see, when I resonate to anger, shame, hatred, or revenge, I add to these decidedly nonspiritual energies by joining in what I find to be so objectionable. But when I remember to bring nonjudgment, love, tolerance, and compassion to these low, ego-dominated energies, I see how different the world looks, and even how different those around me act in the presence of these God-realized energies. I feel optimistic when I'm in-Spirit, with an inner knowing that nothing can interfere with an idea whose time is coming or has already arrived.

I trust that our Creator knows what It's doing, and that good triumphs over what ego believes is bad or evil. I sense that we're all moving toward a world that will no longer know the horrors of war or practice our long-established habits of inhumanity toward our brothers and sisters around the globe, who may have different cultural views and their own unique physical distinctiveness. By staying in-Spirit, I'm truly inspired to see the potential for greatness that's in all of us, as one people, and I turn from anguish to faith that at least I can live from a place of God-realization, and practice being a force for good (God).

Staying in vibrational alignment with Spirit allows me to be more present in all of my life activities. I find myself less concerned with goals, outcomes, winning, and accumulations, and far more involved in the process of enjoying the activities of my life. Arriving seems to replace striving, and being in a state of flow is far more common that my old uninspired state of worry and anguish. I remind myself that Spirit is only here and now—not yesterday, not tomorrow, only *now*. By keeping my vibration aligned spiritually, I see the ecstasy in the present. Everything else that once was a source of worry doesn't come up for me, since the outcomes are already handled for me in my own mind. *What will be, will be,* I remind myself. The world looks so much more peaceful when I approach it this way, and my ego, which once needed to win at all costs, is relegated to a distant seat in a stadium in another galaxy!

Choosing Inspiration

My experience with Jack, as well as many similar kinds of episodes in my life, taught me the that the laws of the material world truly do not apply in the presence of God-realization. And I know that I have the choice to live at this level of inspiration. When I do so, it seems that the world changes: Animals behave differently than their biological genetics would seem to allow, people at a distance seem to hear me telepathically and respond to my highest thoughts, objects seem to materialize in defiance of what scientists say is possible, and healing takes place in spite of modern medicine saying otherwise. In other words, miracles seem to be ordinary. The world looks like a place where everything is possible, where restrictions and limitations are nonexistent, and where the power of our Creator seems to roll right up and land at my feet, begging me to hop on board and witness the infinite possibilities it offers. This is how I feel when I align myself to Spirit: cocky inside because I know something that so few ever come to realize, but humble and awestruck on the outside at the miraculousness of it all!

When I remember to stay in-Spirit, I've realized that when one thing appears to be going wrong, I can see clearly that ten things are going right. For example, if my cell phone isn't working, I can note that my health is fine, my family is safe, the ocean is calm for swimming, my bank account has a surplus, my electricity is fully functional, and on and on it goes. From a perspective of being in-Spirit, I automatically shift my attention away from what's going wrong and onto what's right—this then becomes my point of attraction and I attract more of what I'm focused on, whereas at an earlier time in my life, I'd attract more of what was going wrong because that was my point of attraction. How sublimely beautiful the world now looks to me from this magnificent place of inspiration! No longer do I stay focused on and attract more of what's going wrong, for I've learned to place my attention on what's right, what's working, and what's aligned with the All-Creating Spirit.

From this place of inspiration, I ask, "What if I looked deep within myself and found no original sin at all—that is, what if I discovered original *innocence* instead? And what if the same were true for everyone?" I know that our Creative Source is One of good, and I also know that we must be just like what we came from—therefore, everyone, including myself, is a piece of God. We come to this world from innocence and love, not from a place of sin or weakness. When I see Christ consciousness in everyone, even those with whom I differ greatly, I'm able to feel good (God). When I know that there's no original sin in anyone, I'm able to think like Mother Teresa, who told the world, "In each [ill person], I see the face of Christ in one of his more distressing disguises."

When it is goodness that I look for, rather than sin and weakness, that's what I see. I then see goodness in the little old lady driving slowly in front of me, the elderly man fumbling with his change and delaying me at the supermarket, the children squealing loudly as I'm attempting to concentrate on a book, the teenagers shouting along with their earsplitting rap music, or the jackhammer operator whose deafening sounds fill the air with chaos. When I'm inspired, I see God-realization disguised as a minor blip, and the world looks fine, happy, and even peaceful. I remind myself of Rumi's sage advice: "If you are irritated by every rub, how will you be polished?"

When I feel inspired, I notice how much zest I have for life and everything that I do: I play tennis with exuberance and without fatigue, I write from my heart—I feel good (God), and this inner feeling radiates outward in all of my waking moments. Inspiration means doing what I love, and even more significantly, loving what I'm doing. It's my willingness to bring love and passion to the activities of my life, rather than looking for love to emerge from those events and activities. It's an attitude, and knowing this, I remember to pick a good one as often as possible. I know that being enthusiastic feels good (God), and I also know that I have the choice to select these attitudes at any and all times. When I stay in-Spirit, these outlooks on life become second nature to me.

By deciding to live an inspired life, I'm choosing to be in balance with a Creative Force that responds to my in-Spirit thoughts. I'm also believing that I live in a friendly Universe rather than an evil one, and feeling supported by It in a similar manner. Being grateful for all that God sends my way, I'm not surprised when synchronistic events happen in my life. When I have someone on my mind who lives some distance from me, I actually expect that he or she will call me . . . and it occurs over and over.

I know that thoughts are energy and that those harmonizing with Spirit will align to activate the creation process. I love watching all this flow so perfectly and being in harmony with the Force that's responsible for all of creation. I know deep within me that I can participate in the activation of this Force to bring into reality

248

the manifestation of my spiritually aligned desires.

Rather than hoping, wishing, and even praying for an outcome, my inner world aligns with the idea that what I desire is feasible and on its way. This kind of inspired knowing frees me from anxiety and worry. I affirm: *It's on its way; there's absolutely nothing to fuss about.* And I leave the time of its arrival into my life in the hands of the All-Knowing, Always-Creative Spiritual Source. I find that I no longer question the Creator of the Universe because I'm at peace with the timing of everything. I know enough now not to push the river, not to demand that the timetable of my ego be the same as God's.

I know that by staying in-Spirit, I'm actually participating as a co-creator, and that the more I stay in this aligned space, the more it seems to speed up the process. I've noticed that ever since I've become more conscious of staying inspired (and all that this implies), the time between what I think and having it actually show up in my physical life has become shorter and shorter. I'm aware that the ultimate in manifestation is a complete absence of any delay between a thought and its physical manifestation. What's been called the "gift of loaves and fishes" is what true, 100 percent God-realization is. That is, think food and it appears; think well-being for anyone, and disease dissolves. While I know that this Christ consciousness is available for us all, I have many more glimpses of it as I stay more in-Spirit.

Singing My Song

The major change that's taken place for me in this manifestation of my inspired desires has been the awareness of my own capacity for activating the Creative Force to work with me. Today, as I live consciously in-Spirit, I feel as if I'm more and more able to be an activator of this Divine Synchronistic Force and have it work *with* me, rather than *to* me. I view these mystical moments as holy instants when my ego is suspended, and Spirit (in conjunction with my own Divine desires) has become the teacher.

As my sense of inspiration grows within me, I find myself wanting to do more for others and focusing less upon myself. What I desire is realized through the paradoxical means of desiring it for others even more than I want it for myself. By reaching out in this way and deliberately looking for ways to inspire others, I feel closer and closer to Spirit—and, ironically, I sense that more of what I desire seems to be flowing back to me as a result of this sharing.

At this point in my life I feel that staying in this glorious state of inspiration practically requires me to avoid condemning others. I look at the behaviors of others, even those whose actions are anathema to an inspired world, and I send them love. I know deep within me that declaring war on the problems of violence, poverty, cancer, AIDS, and drug addiction isn't the solution. I'm uninterested in increasing those problems with violent, angry, or hateful thoughts or behavior. I know that I can't get sick enough to make one person better, or angry enough to end violence anywhere. I also sense very strongly that by staying in-Spirit and bringing a higher mental energy to the presence of these lower, ego-based energies, I'm a force for change, one that helps move the world closer to Spirit.

I anticipate a planet at peace—along with health, abundance, and love in my life and in the lives of all others—and I know that it's moving in this direction. I know that for every act of apparent evil, there are a million acts of kindness. That's where I place my attention, and that's what I choose to give away. By doing so for the larger percentage of my days, my reward is a feeling of being in harmony with purpose. I watch the myna birds singing every morning, and I know they're not doing it because they have the answers to all of life's problems—they have a song inside of them that they obviously feel compelled to let come out. I too have a song to sing, and by staying in-Spirit I'm able to sing it all day, every day.

I know that the answer to "What should I be doing?" is to see the word *yes* on my inner screen: "Yes, I am listening"; "Yes, I am paying attention"; and most important, "Yes, I am willing." I notice that those around me who feel uninspired are unwilling to say yes to the feeling at the core of their being. By doing so to every hunch, burning desire, and thought that won't go away, I feel the hand of a guiding Spirit that's with me simply because I've been willing to say yes. By saying yes to life, I see the world and all of its inhabitants in a completely new way.

As a result of being more and more inspired, I see Spirit in virtually everyone I meet. And I feel much more connected to everyone as a result of sensing *their* spirit instead of noticing all of the accumulations of success that they've amassed. I call this "seeing with my mind and not my eyes." It now seems that my identity is associated with experiences that are not exclusively of this world. And I love what my mind sees—possibilities and openings for miracles! It looks past the limitations of my eyes, and it knows that we're all one in an infinite world. My mind no longer views death as something to fear; rather, it lives in an infinite place and is able to step back from this corporeal world and be an observer. With each passing day, I feel what my mind knows to be true, and I look for this all-encompassing loving essence everywhere.

* * *

Adequately conveying how I feel when I'm inspired is probably impossible. What I so sincerely want to share here is that the feeling of being completely in harmony with our Source generates miracles everywhere. I have the delicious spine-tingling sensation of bliss as I observe and interact in this world from the wondrous vista of being inspired. These words from *A Course in Miracles* ring true for me: "All that must be recognized, however, is that birth was not the beginning, and death is not the end." This is the knowing that I have from this infinite in-Spirit perspective.

There are no conflicts—all is as it should be. The things I wish to improve aren't going to be accomplished by fighting, but by placing my attention on staying connected to Spirit. In 1 Corinthians, Saint Paul says, "The very fact that you have lawsuits among you means you have been completely defeated already." As I live from a place of inspiration, I see that conflict is no longer possible for me, and I understand what Paul was attempting to say to the people of Corinth in that letter. I will not be defeated—I can't, because for me, there's no *they* any longer, there's only *us*. I've turned my mind to Spirit. I know that God created me to be like Him, and I must be what I came from. This idea, more than any other, inspires me beyond what I can share on these pages.

It's my intention to continue to stay inspired and live what my mind knows, rather than only what my eyes see. And my mind knows that we're all in a Universe that has a creative, organizing intelligence supporting it. I know that it flows through me, and God willing, I'll stay in-Spirit and assist you to live that life of inspiration that you came here to live. There can be no greater blessing!

I send you love, I surround you with light, and I invite you to live with me in-Spirit.

ABOUT THE AUTHOR

Wayne W. Dyer, Ph.D., is an internationally renowned author and speaker in the field of self-development. He's the author of 28 books; has created many audio programs and videos; and has appeared on thousands of television and radio shows. This book, as well as *Manifest Your Destiny, Wisdom of the Ages, There's a Spiritual Solution to Every Problem,* and *The New York Times* bestsellers *10 Secrets for Success and Inner Peace* and *The Power of Intention,* have all been featured as National Public Television specials in the USA.

Dyer holds a doctorate in educational counselling from Wayne State University and was an associate professor at St. John's University in New York.

Website: **www.DrWayneDyer.com**

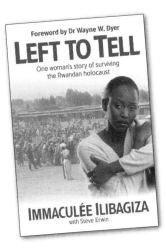

HAY HOUSE TITLES
OF RELATED INTEREST

The Amazing Power of Deliberate Intent: Living the <u>Art of Allowing</u>,
by Esther and Jerry Hicks (The Teachings of Abraham)

*Angel Numbers: The Angels Explain the Meaning of
111, 444, and Other Numbers in Your Life,*
by Doreen Virtue, Ph.D., and Lynnette Brown

Ask and It Is Given: Learning to Manifest Your Desires,
by Esther and Jerry Hicks (The Teachings of Abraham)

The God Code: The Secret of Our Past, the Promise of Our Future,
by Gregg Braden

Gratitude: A Way of Life, by Louise L. Hay and Friends

Power vs. Force: The Hidden Determinants of Human Behavior,
by David R. Hawkins, M.D., Ph.D.

Silent Power, by Stuart Wilde

✳ ✳ ✳

All of the above are available at your local bookstore, for more information visit:
www.hayhouse.co.uk

✳ ✳ ✳

We hope you enjoyed this Hay House book.
If you would like to receive a free catalogue featuring additional
Hay House books and products, or if you would like information
about the Hay Foundation, please contact:

Hay House UK Ltd
Unit 62, Canalot Studios • 222 Kensal Rd • London W10 5BN
Tel: (44) 20 8962 1230; Fax: (44) 20 8962 1239
www.hayhouse.co.uk

***

Published and distributed in the United States of America by:
Hay House, Inc. • PO Box 5100 • Carlsbad, CA 92018-5100
Tel: (1) 760 431 7695 or (800) 654 5126;
Fax: (1) 760 431 6948 or (800) 650 5115
www.hayhouse.com

Published and distributed in Australia by:
Hay House Australia Ltd • 18/36 Ralph St • Alexandria NSW 2015
Tel: (61) 2 9669 4299 • Fax: (61) 2 9669 4144
www.hayhouse.com.au

Published and distributed in the Republic of South Africa by:
Hay House SA (Pty) Ltd • PO Box 990 • Witkoppen 2068
Tel/Fax: (27) 11 706 6612 • orders@psdprom.co.za

Distributed in Canada by:
Raincoast • 9050 Shaughnessy St • Vancouver, BC V6P 6E5
Tel: (1) 604 323 7100 • Fax: (1) 604 323 2600

***

Sign up via the Hay House UK website to receive the Hay House
online newsletter and stay informed about what's going on with
your favourite authors. You'll receive bimonthly announcements
about discounts and offers, special events, product highlights,
free excerpts, giveaways, and more!
www.hayhouse.co.uk